Joel, I really _____ in
your participati_____
wedding. We _____
you and wan_____
of your dreams _____ ____ .

FREE TO
DREAM

Believe in yourself
and remember who you
belong to.

Love
Frederick
James

FREE TO DREAM

NEVA COYLE

BETHANY HOUSE PUBLISHERS
MINNEAPOLIS, MINNESOTA 55438

Published by Bethany House Publishers
A Ministry of Bethany Fellowship, Inc.
6820 Auto Club Road, Minneapolis, Minnesota 55438

Printed in the United States of America

Library of Congress Cataloging-in-Publication Data

Coyle, Neva, 1943–
   Free to dream / Coyle, Neva
      p. cm.

    1. Dreams—Religious aspects—Christianity. 2. Dreams in
the Bible.
I. Title.
BF1078.C695   1990
248.4—dc20   90–39168
ISBN 0–87123–997–3   CIP

To my friends at Yucaipa First Assembly of God, with my thanks and love, I dedicate this book: to the group of women who prayed me through the stages of writing; to the patient and tolerant church members who gave me interviews and unselfishly shared their own wishes and dreams; to those who stopped to ask how this project was going and encouraged me to keep at it.

NEVA COYLE is Founder of Overeaters Victorious and President of Neva Coyle Ministries. Her ministry is enhanced by her bestselling books, tapes, and teaching seminars. Neva and her husband make their home in California.

She may be contacted at:

P.O. Box 2330
Orange, CA 92669

Special Thanks

One of the most hazardous jobs in the world must be editing books. Thanks, Carol and Charette, for having the courage to make me rewrite this book and for having the patience to teach me some new skills. And to Evelyn Bence, for your help and talents at the last.

The second most hazardous job must be working for an author. Writing a book, like constructing a large building, requires that those involved work in a hard-hat area. Thanks, Dede, Jean, and Julie, for being such a support during this time.

It is also hazardous to be married to or to live with an author. Thanks to Lee and the kids. With the completion of this book I can reenter conversations, finish sentences, remember your names, and occasionally cook once again. At least until I begin the next one. . . .

Books by Neva Coyle:

Free To Be Thin, w/Marie Chapian, a successful weight-loss plan which links learning how to eat with how to live

Free to Dream, biblical insights on wishes, dreams, and goals

There's More To Being Thin Than Being Thin, w/ Marie Chapian, focusing on the valuable lessons learned on the *journey* to being thin

Slimming Down and Growing Up, w/Marie Chapian, applying the "Free To Be Thin" principles to kids

Living Free, her personal testimony

Daily Thoughts on Living Free, a devotional

Scriptures for Living Free, a counter-top display book of Scriptures to accompany the devotional

Free To Be Thin Cookbook, a collection of tasty, nutritious recipes complete with the calorie content of each

Free To Be Thin Leader's Kit, a step-by-step guide for organizing and leading an Overeaters Victorious group, including five cassette tapes of instruction

Free To Be Thin Daily Planner, a three-month planner for recording daily thoughts, activities and calorie intake

Getting Your Family On Your Side, how a dieter's family and close friends influence weight-management's successes and failures

Dear Jessica,

Be free, little one, to dream. You *can* become what God designed you to be.

Love,
Grandma N.

Well, I am glad of my dream,
for I hope ere long to see it fulfilled,
to the making of me laugh again.

JOHN BUNYAN

Table of Contents

Introduction

Do you have everything you want? Have you become exactly what you dreamed you would be? Have your prayers been answered specifically and without delay? Is your life totally satisfying right now? Or are you like most of us, living with ghosts of "what might have been" and "if only"?

This book is designed for my Christian sisters who feel trapped in the past or present and have a hard time looking ahead into the future with real hope. They have forgotten that wishes precede reality, that "Faith is being sure of what we hope for and certain of what we do not see" (Hebrews 11:1).

In the pages of this book I trust you will see that you have God's permission to dream. The Word of God is filled with stories of people who wished, hoped, dreamed. But the Bible is a reality book, not a wish book. These dreamers saw those wishes fulfilled as they looked to God for guidance and strength and then stepped out in obedience to His voice. Their stories can become yours.

In 2 Corinthians 6:1 Paul refers to himself and other Christians as "God's fellow workers," and that idea is key to the process of turning vague wishes or discontentment into a satisfying future.

Some might tell you that if wishes become reality it's because the individual takes full responsibility. They think that God is up there somewhere, doing whatever it is He does, and we are down here doing our best to get or become what we want.

That line of thinking is reflected in the over-quoted thought: *What I am is God's gift to me; what I become is my gift to Him.* It's as if God gives us the raw material and then backs up to see what we will do with it. We're basically on our own.

At the other extreme, people seem to think that once you become a Christian you never again have any say or responsibility. They resign themselves to defeat by saying, "Oh well, if God had wanted that for me, He would have worked it out."

In reality, God is with us—giving directions and guidelines—but also asking us to do our part to make our wishes come true.

I have written this book to help you identify your wishes and dreams, bring them to God for confirmation, and clarify the path on which you should walk if those wishes are to be realized.

As you progress through the chapters, you will want to take notes and make lists. You'll want to have a package of three-by-five cards available. I also suggest that you get a ring-binder or spiral-bound notebook and apply the principles presented to your own situation. In the weeks and months to come you can look back and see how far you have progressed in your journey.

In the back of the book I've included several worksheets that you may want to adapt for your needs. I've also compiled a detailed suggested reading list to help you gain additional insights that will encourage you.

This book is for *you*, the woman of this generation, who is asking hard questions:

- Am I all that I was designed to be?
- If not, is there still time?
- Do I have talents I am burying?
- Do I have the desire and energy to move above the status quo?
- Where do I go from here?

May God guide you carefully, step by step, in His loving way. May He draw out of the depths of your being the dreams He planted there, causing them to blossom and bear fruit, for His glory and your delight!

PART

ONE

Identify Your Dreams

*Delight yourself in the Lord and he will give
you the desires of your heart.*
PSALM 37:4

CHAPTER ONE

I've Forgotten How to Dream

Driving through the countryside with a close friend, I popped a question that has become dear to my heart. "What do you wish for?" I asked.

"Not much," Jan replied without hesitation.

"Really?" I knew her well, and I knew she had dreams. "What did you wish for as a child?"

"I didn't want much as a child either," she said.

Wait a minute, I thought, *everyone has wishes— though they might be buried.* I tried harder to unearth hers. "What did you pretend when you were a little girl?"

Her voice became animated, and I knew I'd hit something. "I pretended I could fly," she reminisced, obviously amused.

"You did?"

"Yes, I always wished I could be a pilot."

"Me too," I said, and we laughed together.

Jan grew quiet for a short while, and I was able to let my mind wander back to my own childhood.

Most of my childhood dreams were pure flight-of-fancy, spilling out of a mind and heart that were free to wander at will. I wanted, for instance, to have long blond hair like Queen Aleta in the "Prince Valiant" comic strips. I didn't have a bicycle of my own, so I dreamed of having not just one, but a different bicycle for each school day. Other dreams had some root in reality, but were blocked because of some fear or resistance in me. Like the dream of being able to ride a horse the way Elizabeth Taylor did in the movie *National Velvet*, when I was really intimidated by the family pony. Others came from idealizing what my future would be like: I played house with furniture I had made from orange crates and curtains made out of printed chicken-feed sacks, and my children were perfectly obedient babydolls or else imaginary little angels.

Some dreams did come true, after a bit of careful planning and work—like the time I absolutely couldn't live without a "Sparkle Plenty" doll. Sparkle Plenty was a wonderful character in the Dick Tracy comic strips, and one day I came across an ad from a toy manufacturer offering this look-alike doll by mail order. My heart did a somersault! For weeks after, my mother helped me raise money for that special doll by giving me all the soda pop bottles for refunding. My grandpa also saw to it that I got a quarter or two each week—until finally all my amassed "wealth" was cashed in for a money order and sent off. I will never forget the day that package arrived by mail and was placed in my eager hands. . . .

Jan broke into my private reverie, "I also pretended I could run fast and jump high. I wanted to be a track star. My mother would get so angry when I would drag a mattress outside, under a window. I'd go back inside and jump onto it.

"I also wished I could have long, straight hair. My hair was so curly. The snarls nearly killed me every time my mother tried to brush them out."

Just as I'd expected, Jan had needed only a little prodding to remember. "I thought you didn't have any wishes when you were young," I said.

"I guess I'd forgotten, but when you asked what I pretended, the dreams came back. It's funny, now that I remember them, I can even feel them, as if they were still part of me."

"Did you ever pretend as a teenager?"

"Yeah. I pretended I was popular; I acted my way through high school. I flirted with all the boys and pretended I could get any boyfriend I wanted. In reality I was never asked out, but I pretended it was because none of them ever suited me." She paused. "A relationship probably would have scared me to death."

Like Jan, my dreams also changed when I'd reached adolescence.

For one thing, there seemed to be an element of tension added to my dreams.

I was beginning to feel, for instance, that I wanted to *help* people. This was more than a nice sentiment, it was a definite push or need inside of me. I considered nursing, counseling, mission work, but none of these goals seemed possible—first, because college wasn't high on my family's priority list and, second, because a young woman's highest (and in those days, almost only) goal was to become a housewife and mother.

But the nagging desire to help change lives would not go away. . . .

My attention turned back to Jan beside me in the front seat of my car. "What do you pretend now?"

"I don't pretend," she said. I detected a catch in her voice.

"Do you have dreams now?"

"Yes," she said, almost whispering. "I guess so. But they're too painful to talk about."

"Do you think of them often?"

"I try not to."

"What do you do with them?"

"I push them away, unless someone—like you—prods me."

In some way, I sensed she was giving me permission to keep prodding, so I asked, "How do you push away your dreams?"

"I pretend they don't exist. Sometimes I fill my schedule so tight I don't have to think of what I really want. I also try to help other people fulfill their dreams; I feel better when I see other people happy. My husband. My kids. . . ." But her voice trailed off, as if she really didn't believe what she was saying either.

Forgetting What It's Like

I don't think my friend is the only one who's lost touch with her wishes and dreams.

I know women who organize a detailed list of household chores on three-by-five cards. On calendars they write scrupulous accounts of activities and appointments. They make and keep shopping lists. They have detailed inventories of all the family belongings. Yet if asked to name (say nothing of writing down or prioritizing) their own hearts' desires or untapped abilities, they'd step back in retreat.

Something happens to many people—especially women—when they pass over some imaginary line that separates youth from adulthood. They forget what it's like to dream.

In 1 Corinthians 13 the apostle Paul said that he'd put away childish things. He may have put wishing behind him in that "star-light, star-bright" sense, the way a child hopes that someone else will magically grant his or her wishes by morning. But the letters of Paul witness to a life that was full of more healthy desires for which he vigorously worked, prayed, and greatly sacrificed.

What does it mean to dream—in the *wishing* sense? *Webster's New World Dictionary* defines the verb *wish* as "to have a longing for; want; desire. To long; yearn."

A healthy wish propels us into the future—the minutes, days, months, and years ahead that are now beyond our sight. But why do some of us look ahead into the future and see little to wish for?

When the Past Taints the Future

Like my friend Jan, many people have lost touch with their dreams because they seem painful. Maybe they feel like Antoine de Saint Exupery, who describes a negative, it's-too-late view:

> Nobody grasped you by the shoulder while there was still time. Now the clay of which you were shaped has hardened and naught in you will ever waken the sleeping musician, the poet, the astronomer that possibly inhabited you in the beginning.

The "reasons" for giving up our dreams are numerous: "I was born on the wrong side of the tracks"; "My parents or teachers never encouraged me"; "If I'd studied more in school . . . but I didn't, so now I'll never be able to . . ."; "I've never had any physical stamina"; "If I hadn't had these kids when I was so young. . . ."; "If I had enough time—or money. . . ."

Sometimes we blame our own past sins for our inability to dream. "If only I hadn't had to get married. . . ."

Discouraging Words

Maybe you shared your most heartfelt wishes with people who outright discouraged you: "You don't really think you can . . ."; "There's no way . . ."; "Yeah, I've heard that before . . ."; "You're young, and you'll think differently when you get older"; "And just where do you think you'll get the money for that? Dad and I aren't rich, you know."

Some have even suffered attacks against their very character. One brilliant woman I know is the daughter of Polish immigrants who came to this country in the 1940s. Marjorie watched her high school classmates go off to college in the 1950s, while she was told, "You could never make it in college." Sadly, she is now retiring after twenty years as a secretary at a university where she could have taken courses free of charge—but never sat through one lecture because of the words so long ago that burst her dream.

Disillusionment

Disillusionment is the dream killer of all time. Ever hear someone who had an "every-silver-lining-has-a-cloud" view on life? "I had a few dreams come true when I was younger, and they weren't at all what I expected. The disappointment of finding what I thought I wanted wasn't so great after all—well, it was more than I want to face again. I'll just be easy from now on and take what comes."

When any of these painful memories or emotions crops up, the path of least resistance beckons. It's easiest to run from the pain, flight which usually includes burying our dreams—any dreams.

Some dreams are not all we have built them up to be. When my husband Lee was young, he dreamed of being a mechanic. In high school he was elated when he found himself a job as a mechanic's helper.

But suddenly he was breathing gas fumes by the hour. Now he can laugh (though he didn't then) about lying under a car one winter and having a chunk of ice fall into his face. The reality of the dream was more like a nightmare to him, so he chose a different career. He refused to walk the pessimistic path of disillusionment with life.

When Fear Keeps Us From Wishing

Whether based on past failure or an imagined future, our fear of failure can stop us cold. I know I've sometimes reacted to kernels of wishes with fear. "I just couldn't carry through with it."

But you and I aren't the first to come up with excuses for not becoming all we could become, nor are our excuses original.

Remember the story of Moses at the burning bush? God told Moses that he would be a spokesman to deliver his people from slavery, and Moses shrank from it. After receiving sign after sign of God's power, Moses says, "O Lord, I have never been eloquent, neither in the past nor since you have spoken to your servant. I am slow of speech and tongue" (Exodus 4:10).

I couldn't say it better than did Francis Bacon: "It is a miserable state of mind to have few things to desire, and many things to fear."

When "More Important Things" Keep Us From Wishing

Some people have shut down their wishing because so many other things seem so much more important.

Sometimes the logic goes like this: Those around me—or even far away in Africa—are in such need. How can I rationalize any of my wishes when I should be more concerned about their needs?

I know one woman who felt guilty about wanting to lose weight while her friend was dying of cancer. She somehow thought that her friend's struggle to hold on to life discounted her own dream and made it seem frivolous—not that staying overweight could make her friend get well.

The comparison trap grips especially tight when the "other party" is family. So many women are tempted to think, "My husband's—or children's—needs are more important than mine."

The internal conflict may not decrease much when the children leave home. One woman I know has grown children who are struggling financially. She knows it isn't wise to continually bail them out of tight spots, but their situations make her feel guilty for spending any money on herself. As far as she is concerned, her own dreams are shelved indefinitely, until her children get on their feet.

A variation on this "someone-is-more-important-than-me" theme is played by the woman who tries to make sure her husband is in the lead— tries so hard, in fact, that she gives up her gifts and talents and personal goals. Some women find it hard to believe that anything good or worthwhile could come to them or from them, just because they are women.

But things get more complicated when we feel guilty for being anything less than perfectly content. Aren't we told to be thankful—and content—in all things? In *Inside Out* Larry Crabb notes:

> Often, when Christian people admit to themselves that they're wanting something, they immediately feel selfish. "I'm just thinking of myself. I know I shouldn't be concerned with whether things go my way. I should care more about the needs of others." And so they pray God will help them get over their selfishness.

Have We Forgotten?

How is it that we've forgotten the stories of the biblical wishers? There was Queen Esther, whose fulfilled dream saved her endangered nation. There was widowed Naomi, who put aside her bitterness to look ahead and wish for a future generation. There was Deborah who rose to meet the need of the hour. There were Hannah, Sarah, and Elizabeth, whose prayers God heard, and the hemorrhaging woman who sought Jesus' healing.

You Are Important to God

You see, we are important to God. We—whether male or female—are made in God's image: "So God created man in his own image, in the image of God he created him; male and female he created them" (Genesis 1:27).

Time after time in the Bible, God showed His love to His daughters. One amazing story is found in 1 Kings 17. There's a famine in the land and a widow of Zarephath is gathering sticks when the prophet Elijah asks her for a piece of bread. Beyond all hope, she states her case, "I don't have any bread—only a handful of flour in a jar and a little oil in a jug. I am gathering a few sticks to take home and make a meal for myself and my son, that we may eat it—and die" (v. 12).

Elijah persists and tells her that if she will make bread and give him the first piece, the Lord will daily replenish her oil and meal until the drought ends. When the woman heeds Elijah's request, the Lord fulfills His promise. But there's more to the story. Some time later, the woman's son grows ill and dies. Again embittered she lashes out at Elijah, who miraculously restores the boy to life.

That woman and her heartache were important to God . . . and so was the outcast Samaritan woman Jesus met at the well . . . as are you and I. Men have no corner on God's love, and women have no corner on feeling unworthy of it. Jesus summed up His feeling of compassion toward those who consider themselves insignificant: "Are not five sparrows sold for two pennies? Yet not one of them is forgotten by God. Indeed, the very hairs of your head are all numbered. Don't be afraid; you are worth more than many sparrows" (Luke 12:6–7).

Your Wishes Are Important to God

As Larry Crabb says, "We can't deny our inside desires without losing touch with a very real part of ourselves." Psalm 37:4 says our identity is tied to our dreams: "Delight yourself in the Lord and he will give you the desires of your heart ("*leb*")."

Throughout the Old Testament the nouns *leb* and *lebab* ("heart") refer to the very core of a person or thing, such as the sea. In this psalm David is referring to the desires that we carry deep in our beings—the desires that are part of our very identity.

If we are important to God, our wishes are important to Him. The verse that best reminds me of this is Psalm 138:8: "The Lord will fulfill his purpose for me," or as the King James Version puts it, "The Lord will perfect that which concerneth me."

The Lord does have a plan: "For we are God's workmanship, created in Christ Jesus to do good works, which God prepared in advance for us to do" (Ephesians 2:10). Some of our dreams are implanted by Him to further His plan, and to fulfill a precious promise He made to each one of us: "I have come that they may have life, and have it to the full" (John 10:10).

Looking Back to Look Ahead

Before we continue this first section, exploring specific ways you can identify your wishes, let's take one more look at the past—the weight that drags us down and keeps us from considering the future.

Hebrews 12:1 admonishes believers to "throw off everything that hinders and the sin that so easily entangles." That includes our past disappointments, failures, sins, and doubts. Then the scripture continues, "Let us run with perseverance the race marked out for us. Let us fix our eyes on Jesus, the author and perfecter of our faith. . . ."

A friend of mine has told me of her life before her conversion. She came to Christ because her life was futile and hopeless. Though she still occasionally wonders if Jesus can really love someone with a past like hers, she keeps reminding herself that those sins are behind the cross.

My friend's story is not mine. I was raised in a Christian home, having accepted Christ as a child, and never dramatically rebelled. I don't have a "vivid" past that haunts me. And yet I have failed my Lord time and again. There have been days when I wondered if He could love me any longer or if my personal failures had disqualified me for ministry.

I've learned that repentance is not just for the unsaved. For Christians it must be a lifestyle. As we confess our sins, God is faithful to forgive and purify us. That promise—1 John 1:9—was written to believers. While we might experience a setback and need time for restoration, we are forgiven. With the cross between us and our sin, we are fresh like the dawn and ready to look to the future. Though innocence is never returned to us, cleanliness is.

An Invitation

Note the invitation our Lord gives you:

"Come now, let us reason together," says the Lord. "Though your sins are like scarlet, they shall be as white as snow; though they are red as crimson, they shall be like wool." (Isaiah 1:18)

Come to me, all you who are weary and burdened, and I will give you rest. (Matthew 11:28)

As you prayerfully look at your own past, turn to the first page of your Dreams Notebook and write a heading across the top: Reasons Why I Find It Hard to Dream. If this chapter has helped you identify any reasons why your wishing seems to have become blocked, write them down. Be as specific as possible. Has "hope deferred" made your heart sick? Has sin blocked your vision for the future? Has guilt weighed you down?

Now, across each reason you have identified, write in big capital letters GOD IS GREATER. The past *is* in the hands of the God of hope and love. It is no longer yours to hide behind or to use as an excuse for not dreaming.

As I have learned to write GOD IS GREATER over my past, I've gained new insights into who I am as a daughter of God. I've also learned to walk ahead into the future, trusting in His love.

I ask you to allow our heavenly Father this chance to resurrect His dreams within you— whether they lie half-buried or broken. Let His Holy Spirit search your heart. And, as you think and pray through the simple exercises on these pages, allow yourself to become more of the person you always dreamed you could be!

CHAPTER TWO

The Heart of the Matter

> We cannot fool ourselves for long about what we are to do. Somewhere deep down in us is stored the secret, and when we are digging in the wrong place, we know it. The secret wants to be discovered and will not let us go in peace a way that is not ours.
>
> —Elizabeth O'Connor
> *The Eighth Day of Creation*

Whether or not we can name them on demand, our hopes and dreams are inside us, waiting to be brought to light. Even the process of finding them can be an adventure as we discover threads of meaning and potential woven throughout our life!

Without dreams we become stagnant—bored, dull, and unproductive. Vague, unfulfilled wishes take up emotional room, crowding out new wishes and making us doubt. But God wants us to feel the excitement of His promise: " 'I know the plans I have for you,' declares the Lord, 'plans to prosper you and not to harm you, plans to give you hope and a future' " (Jeremiah 29:11).

The Royal Court

Consider this scene from the Bible: A lovely girl in her mid-teens dons her most stunning gown and jewels. She leaves her room, crosses an outer courtyard, and silently stands in the inner court, in sight of her king sitting on his throne. She chooses a specific spot in the sunlight, which makes her hair sheen and her creamy skin glow.

At the sight of his young queen, the king quickens. Without a word he slowly, yet eagerly extends to her his royal scepter. She drops her eyes and walks gracefully toward him, reaching out her hand and touching the tip of the scepter.

The king loves her. He sees how she has dressed to please him, and his heart races.

In a low voice he asks, "What is your request? Up to half of my kingdom, I will give you, Esther." His eyes search her flawless face. What will it be? Clothes? Jewels? Caravans? The king has given his word; he will take responsibility for granting anything she wants, up to half of all the splendor that he owns.

She lifts her eyes with confidence, and speaks with simple clarity. "Come with Haman today to a banquet I have prepared," she requests. And in time she makes another request—that the king reverse his decree that her Jewish people be slaughtered.

Center stage, Queen Esther is willing to take responsibility for defining her wishes. But there's a part of the story I left out. Before she went into the king's presence she spent three days praying and fasting. She got away from the distractions that might otherwise have occupied her days. As she quieted herself, she discovered that at the core of her soul lay a destiny, a role that only she could fulfill.

Think of yourself standing before King Jesus, as Esther stood before her king. He does not extend a royal scepter, He extends to you His hand. Imagine covering the scar in His hand with your fingers as you place your hand in His. Hear His sweet words to you: "What is your request?"

Identifying Wishes

To finish a good book, you must read it. To have a clean house, you must get out your duster, mop, and vacuum cleaner and get rid of the dirt. To identify your dreams, you must allow yourself to dream.

Wishing can be a simple mental activity, but I've discovered that writing down thoughts helps me to hold on to them. I can track the progress I've made or see how God leads me in relation to a specific dream. I never set aside time for dreaming without pulling out my Dreams Notebook, ready to write down what comes to mind.

Honesty Is the Best Policy

So much of our lives is spent on the "How are you? I'm fine" level that real honesty seems threatening. But this Dreams Notebook is only for your eyes and God's, and you can trust God with your secrets. As Larry Crabb says:

> Be open to looking at everything in your life. Don't run too quickly from disturbing events. . . . Let your mind explore the hard issues that provoke some really unsettling questions in order to provoke a more trusting awareness of Christ.

We can be open with God. Just read 1 Samuel 1, and you'll see the barren woman Hannah laying out her wish before God. Verse 10–11 says,

> In bitterness of soul Hannah wept much and prayed to the Lord. . . .O Lord Almighty, if you will only look upon your servant's misery and remember me, and not forget your servant but give her a son, then I will. . . .

In her case, the watching priest, Eli, thought her display so out of order that he accused her of being drunk. He noted not only her emotion but "Eli observed her mouth. Hannah was praying in her heart, and her lips were moving but her voice was not heard" (vv. 12–13). You see Hannah was not only taking her emotion to God, she was honestly and earnestly talking to Him!

Gien Karssen notes this: "Hannah didn't pray vaguely. She made a specific request. 'God, I want to have a son.' She talked directly to God." And we can do likewise.

In her book, *Prayer: Conversing with God*, Rosalind Rinker describes a form of prayer I have grown to value. She advises speaking to God in simple, everyday language, as you would address any friend in whom you have a deep level of confidence. Instead of making "prayer-speeches" to

Him, just talk things over with Him. Let the conversation go back and forth, including time for Him to respond, as when having a conversation with a valued friend.

We have a personal God who cares for His creation, especially we who are made in His image. He wants us to communicate with Him, as a parent wants to hear a child.

I began learning how to pray to God out of the deep longing that comes with a lifelong dream the day that one of my daughters shut me out of her life.

When she was fifteen, I received a call one day from her employer, who informed me my daughter was being fired from her summer babysitting job because her boyfriend would not stay away. Nor did she seem interested in discouraging him, which I found out in a hurry when I confronted her at home later. She stormed into her room, slammed the door, and in so doing, shut me out of her heart.

From then on, she shrugged off any physical contact, saying, "You give me the creeps when you touch me." My already-strained attempts to set controls and guidelines for her behavior and privileges were stretched even further: She came home one day with a hickey on her neck; she stayed out past curfew. When we bought her a birthstone ring for her sixteenth birthday, her only reply was, "What a weird gift to get from a parent."

I will share more about this story later. For now, I want to emphasize just this point:

Feeling like such a failure as a parent, I knew

that I could run to One who would not reject me but would accept me as a loved and hurting child—to my heavenly Father.

Psalm 103:13 says, "As a father has compassion on his children, so the Lord has compassion on those who fear him."

The psalms of David are filled with heartfelt cries directed at God. In Psalm 38:9 David says, "All my longings lie open before you, O Lord; my sighing is not hidden from you." Both Hannah and David could be open before the Lord because they trusted Him. There is nothing so deep, so personal, or so important that it cannot be trusted to God, the Lord of the universe who "knows how we are formed" and "remembers that we are dust" (Psalm 103:14).

"For we do not have a high priest who is unable to sympathize with our weaknesses, but we have one who has been tempted in every way, just as we are—yet was without sin. Let us then approach the throne of grace with confidence, so that we may receive mercy and find grace to help us in our time of need" (Hebrews 4:15–16).

In Psalm 119:9, David asks, "How can a young man keep his way pure?" His answer is given in the next phrase: "By living according to your word." The answer is not "By living in secrecy," as if we were even capable of keeping secrets from an omniscient God. Even the atheist Mark Twain said, "You can't pray a lie."

Later we'll examine the validity of wishes and how they might or might not fit in with God's plan for us. But first we have to lay the groundwork.

Set Aside Time

Prayer and Bible reading on a daily basis are fundamental to a victorious Christian life. But I'm asking that you set aside some extra time for several mornings—just to dream. A block of time following your daily quiet time would be perfect. You may have to get up a few minutes earlier than usual, but I guarantee this small sacrifice of sleep will be well worth your effort.

Ask God to direct your thoughts; allow yourself to be aware of the Holy Spirit's presence. Unclutter your mind and quietly meditate before the Lord.

Boldly Explore

In your Dreams Notebook, write dreams that you identify either through your free brainstorming or in response to the following reflective questions. Though you might want to consider only a few questions on the first morning, read through the list so the questions percolate in your subconscious throughout the day and night.

- If I could do anything I wanted, what would I do?
- If I could be anything, what would I be?
- If I could live anywhere, where would I live?
- If I could change anything about myself, what would I change?
- I wouldn't feel so useless if I could just ⸺.

- If I could get control of one fear, what fear would it be?
- If I could repair one relationship, which relationship would it be?
- I would like to have more time to _____ .
- I would like to have more time with _____ .
- I am happiest when I'm _____ .
- I am most restless when I'm _____ .
- I get depressed when I think about _____ .
- People tell me I'm good at _____ .
- If I had the money I would _____ .
- Would I ever enjoy _____ !
- I wanted to be _____ when I grew up.
- When I was in grammar school I pretended to _____ .
- As a child I was happiest when I was _____ (where?) doing _____ (what?).
- My best subject in school was _____ .
- At age _____ I wished I could _____ . (Answer this same question thinking in terms of specific ages. Don't stop when you reach adulthood—age five, eleven, eighteen, twenty-one, thirty-five. . . .)
- I most admire _____ (name) because _____ .
- I envy _____ (name) because _____ .
- When I'm elderly and looking back on my life, I will have regrets if I haven't _____ . (You might also ask this question about five, ten, or twenty years from now.)
- I feel I have untapped talents as a _____ .
- I feel God has given me _____ , and therefore I want to give Him _____ .

As you ponder these questions, thoughts come to your mind that you need to write down immediately, then take a closer look. Is this your *own* dream—or is it what a parent wished for you? Is it your dream—or your husband's desire for you? Try to uncover your own wishes—who do *you* want to be?

Listen to yourself in conversations and observe yourself relating to other people. You might be surprised to hear and "see" some of your wishes surface as you talk.

Record every wish that comes to your mind without judging its merits.

To identify my dreams I periodically read back through my own personal notebooks, extensive journals that include the thoughts and prayers of my daily quiet times. You might try this on a scheduled day of the year—maybe your birthday, New Year's Day, or Valentine's Day. When I review my notebooks, I pull out the dreams I have so randomly written down. I summarize them on one or two pages. If you are a journaler, look back through old journals to see which unfulfilled dreams lie hidden in those pages.

My Story

I've always been a dreamer. I come by it naturally, because my parents were always carving out a new frontier of one sort or another. They built a house from the ground up, started a church in a little desert town that had none, and bought property out in the middle of nowhere because "soon the town will be building out this way and this land will be worth something." Being brought up with that pioneer spirit, I quickly learned how to hold on to wishes.

One basic skill I learned (without even knowing I was being taught) was how to build a *foundation* for a dream. With motherhood and a household of my own still years away, I learned how to systematically make beds, wash dishes, clean house, shop for clothes and groceries on a budget; and I babysat, both for the money and the training. My dream of "helping" was committed to the Lord in prayer and to the counsel of older Christians like my pastor, my Sunday school teacher, and my mother.

Another skill I learned about dream-building was how to *think practically*. As a teenager, with an itch to own a car that would get me places, I instinctively held my dream in one hand (wheels!) and reality (*$$$*) in the other. At last, I set my sights on a Nash Metropolitan, a very little car, inexpensive to operate but sufficient to get me around.

These basic skills, I have found, make the difference between dreams that die and those that slowly, steadily come true.

An Ongoing Process

Though I suggest you set aside extra time for several days to work on this activity, know that the process of uncovering your dreams is ongoing. I expect to be writing in my Dreams Notebook for the rest of my life. As some dreams are fulfilled or die natural deaths, others take their place. As you take your wishes to God and allow Him to work in your life, you're likely to see underlying wishes that are the roots of those first wishes you've identified. Whenever new wishes occur to you, add them to your list.

Whenever you read or think of any scripture that seems in any way relevant to any dream, note it, because God, even at this early stage, will start leading you along His paths. His will doesn't often come by trumpet blasts, but it comes as we seek Him in His Word.

Sorting Your Wishes

Imagine for a minute that your dreams are library books. Some of the books in this library are fiction, as are some of your dreams. Some of the books are for reference, as are some of your wishes—for they hold a wealth of information about your inner being. Some books are specifically written as textbooks, and some dreams are for teaching us lessons.

Some books are thick, some are thin; some are hardbound and some are paper—but the true value of a book is not in the binding and cover, it's in the insight it gives to the reader. Just as each book is valuable, so is each of your wishes, but right now your dreams may well be in disarray, like library books that have been dumped into the after-hours book drop. To be rightly returned to the carefully organized shelves, those books need to be sorted and put in order. It's quite simple to do the same with your dreams.

Clarify

As you collect your scattered dreams on a page or two of a notebook, go on to the next step: write down each one on a separate three-by-five card. Don't simply copy the dream word-for-word from your notebook, reduce it to fifteen words or less, and state it in as clear a way as you can.

Jesus did not request general blessings from the Father. Notice how specific Jesus was in His prayer for His disciples: "I am not praying for the world, but for those you have given me. . . . Holy Father, protect them by the power of your name—the name you gave me—so that they may be one as we are one" (John 17:9, 11).

Further on He said, "My prayer is not that you take them out of the world but that you protect them from the evil one" (v. 15).

Jesus knew what He wanted from His Father and He got right to the point. He wants us to do the same.

Set aside time for several mornings to clarify your wishes. As soon as you write a wish on a card, repeat it aloud, presenting your request to God, speaking to a loving God, telling Him how important the wish is to you. As Rosalind Rinker says, "Somehow it is easy to speak to Jesus Christ. After all, we know that He knows what it feels like to be us."

All my longings lie open before you, O Lord; my sighing is not hidden from you. (Psalm 38:9)

Evaluate

With your cards spread around you, try to see if wishes run in categories. What do certain dreams have in common with others? There may be *I-wish-I-had's* and *I-wish-I-were's* and *I-wish-I-could's*.

Do many of your wishes have to do with relationships? If so, are you harboring one underlying wish for a satisfactory relationship, one that you haven't yet identified and so it lies at the root of these surface wishes? Is it really *that* person you must be with, or is it just that *that* person seems to be your only option for any kind of meaningful relationship?

Is it *that* house that you want, or, as you look at all your wishes, do you see that you simply want a change of scenery? Do many of your wishes have to do with possessions or position? What underlies the dreams?

As you evaluate, you may well discover some dreams that are "fairy-tale wishes" because they aren't based in reality. They don't require anything of you; they don't require that you grow or work for them in any way. Nor do they require you to live by faith, because they're based in a desire to find an easy and quick way out of trouble. "I wish I would inherit a bundle of money from a relative I don't even know I have." "I wish a Hollywood talent scout would discover me at the corner grocery store." "I wish the governor would recognize me as the state's most outstanding citizen." If you see any fairy-tale wishes, try to reword them more reasonably. They might be based in a wish for financial security—or for personal recognition.

As you evaluate, you're likely to discard some cards and add others, refining your wishes.

When you feel you've narrowed them down, categorize your wishes in major life areas. This new arrangement may give you yet another perspective on your life. Areas might include: family life, spiritual life, vocation, Christian ministry, hobbies, physical health, emotional health, social relationships, finances, education. Write the category of each wish in the upper left corner of the card.

Prioritize

Just as all dreams do not surface at the same time, neither can you work on them all at once. So on a scale of one to five, give each dream a rating. A number one dream would be most important to you. A number five would be at the bottom of the pile. Using pencil, so you can reprioritize later, write each dream's rating in the upper right corner of the card.

Place all your number ones in a pile, the twos in another, and so forth. As you read through each category, you might see things differently and want to make adjustments.

You've Only Just Begun

Having identified and sorted through your dreams, you've taken the first step to making them become reality. At this point you've laid out your wishes honestly before yourself and God.

Now it's time to seek the Lord's face more intensely by asking how these dreams fit into His plan for you.

PART

TWO

Sanctify Your Dreams

"Abba, Father," he said, "everything is possible for you. Take this cup from me. Yet not what I will, but what you will."

MARK 14:36

CHAPTER THREE

Here I Am, Lord

Identifying and sorting your wishes is not the same as filling out a catalog order form. Similarly, finding a Scripture verse to support the wish does not automatically guarantee that it's in God's will for you, or that it will come true.

Some people quote John 14:14 as proof that God is obligated to grant any request: "You may ask me for anything in my name, and I will do it." But a single Bible verse shouldn't be viewed out of context any more than a single puzzle piece should be expected to show what the larger picture looks like. That broader context includes the theme of sacrifice: "Any of you who does not give up everything he has cannot be my disciple" (Luke 14:33).

Larry Crabb speaks of wishes this way, "The existence of a desire does not justify its satisfaction." We need to bring every dream to God, not for Him to grant—for us to give. We need to sanctify it in His presence.

What Does It Mean to Sanctify?

Sanctification is really not a difficult concept. It means to present, to offer, to set apart for God's use.

Mary the mother of Jesus summarized it perfectly when she answered the angel of the Lord, "I am the Lord's . . ." (Luke 1:38). In those few words Mary was saying, "My plans and my desires—my life—belong to the Lord."

Right from the beginning of her biblical story, Mary set about aligning herself with God's plan—rather than asking Him to align himself with hers. And right at the beginning the angel assured her, "Nothing is impossible with God" (Luke 1:37).

Hannah did the same even as she made her request for a child known to God. Addressing her prayer to the "Lord Almighty," she acknowledged His power. In contrast to this expression of His *everythingness*, she acknowledged her *nothingness*, calling herself God's servant.

That is what sanctification is about—bowing before the Lord our God. And as we bring ourselves and our wishes to the Lord, He makes His plans known to us.

When we think of *sanctification*, we usually think in terms of sanctifying ourselves and being sanctified. But think about it: If the desires of our hearts are the longings that come from the very center of our beings, then our dreams and our inner *selves* are inseparable. To sanctify our dreams *is* to sanctify ourselves.

Paul prayed a wonderful prayer for the Colossian Christians. This is also my prayer for you as you sanctify your dreams before the Lord:

> Since the day we heard about you, we
> have not stopped praying for you and asking
> God to fill you with the knowledge of his will
> through all spiritual wisdom and under-
> standing. And we pray this in order that you
> may live a life worthy of the Lord and may
> please him in every way: bearing fruit in
> every good work, growing in the knowledge
> of God, being strengthened with all power
> according to his glorious might so that you
> may have great endurance and patience, and
> joyfully giving thanks to the Father, who has
> qualified you to share in the inheritance of
> the saints in the kingdom of light. (Colossians
> 1:9–12)

Setting the Stage for Sanctifying Our Wishes

As I read Hannah's story in 1 Samuel, I see a
pattern in the sanctification of her dream, and I
want to commend it to you.

Set a Time to Be Alone

At the end of the day, after the evening meal,
Hannah slipped away to be alone with God. It is
so easy to get so busy with our responsibilities and
activities that we do not have the time to come
away by ourselves. Many of us are so used to being
spiritually fed at group activities, large meetings,
conferences, and Bible study groups that we
aren't even comfortable being alone with God.

But a personal relationship is not developed
in a group. We need to be alone with Jesus, to

meet Him in ways that cannot happen otherwise.

In a place where I can see it often, I have posted a short quote from Gordon MacDonald's book *Ordering Your Private World*. It reads:

> If my private world is in order, it will be because I am unafraid to be alone and quiet before Christ.

Jesus himself repeatedly left His disciples and the crowds to speak in private with His Father in heaven.

If you are not in the habit of a daily quiet time, I urge you to make a place for this in your schedule. (Maybe "I wish I could have more time with God" was on your wish list anyway.) Early morning works best for me, and it may for you too.

In my daily quiet time I value both freedom *and* structure. That means I pray and meditate. I also plan time for Bible reading and recording both scriptural insights and practical applications for my life in my journal.

To sanctify your dreams I recommend blocks of time for periods of reflection. Why? Because it's often impossible to quiet ourselves quickly. By the time we are quiet and ready to be still in the Lord's presence, the precious time is gone.

In planning for a time alone, set aside enough time to allow for a period of relaxation, staring at the ceiling or sky if necessary, just to clear your mind of distractions. In *Ordering Your Private World*, Gordon MacDonald says it well:

> Many of us will discover that it takes preparatory time in order to meditate. You may have had the experience of coming in from

heavy exercise still breathing very hard. You know that it is virtually impossible to sit down for several minutes and be still. There is too much gasping and the catching of breath for quiet sitting. The same is true in reflection. We often enter the chamber to meet with God while we are still emotionally out of breath. It is hard at first to concentrate our thoughts and to bring them into the presence of the Lord. We have to quietly relax for a short season while the mind accustoms itself to spiritual activity in the "garden" environment. Thus, it will take time—time some people are reluctant to give.

Try to take the better part of a morning, afternoon, or evening to be alone with God. And don't think of this as being a once-in-a-lifetime retreat. Try it once a year or more! Even though I regularly have my daily devotional times at home in the early morning, I find I quickly "wear down" if I don't take special retreats out of my regular routine to be alone with God. Don't worry about family or other significant relationships being hurt by periodic withdrawal to be alone with God. When you return, you will have more to give them.

Select a Place and Establish an Altar

Hannah went to the tabernacle, where she knew she would be assured of God's presence. In the Old Testament, God dwelled in the tabernacle. Since Pentecost, He has chosen to dwell within the hearts of people like you and me. Anywhere you go, God's presence is with and in you.

But even though we do not select a place because God will be there more than He would be any-where else, there are places that are more con-ducive than others to our being aware of His pres-ence within us.

I have several places I go to be alone: a local park set on a hill overlooking an orange grove and some of our historic Victorian homes, my bedroom when my family is away in the middle of the day, the sanctuary of my little church, a little travel-trailer parked year-round in a secured campground thirty minutes from my office.

In each of these places, I establish an altar where I can pour out my heart to God—a picnic table or a park bench, my bed, the altar railing in the front of the church, or outdoors alone at the trailer park.

Become Aware of God's Presence

James 4:8 says that when we draw near to God, He draws near to us. Though God lives deep within us, we are not always aware of His pres-ence.

In this regard, a blind Catholic sister once gave me this advice, "First, become aware of your own breath. Listen to your breathing. Then re-alize that God is even closer to you than your own breath. He is living within you, and just as your breath brings life into your body, God brings life into your spirit."

I love the way Elizabeth O'Connor says it in *The Eighth Day of Creation:*

Center your attention ... deep within

yourself so that what emerges flows from the core of your being, and not from some peripheral point on the circumference of your life where all kinds of distractions and the opinions of others flow in and take you further from yourself.

We do not go deep within to merely find more of ourselves. As Christians, we find God is there, deep within us, not at "some peripheral point on the circumference of life."

Lay Your Wishes Before the Lord

As we discussed in the last chapter, Hannah simply stated her wishes in God's presence: "I want to have a son." And that day Hannah offered herself and her wishes to God: "If you will . . . not forget your servant but give her a son, then I will give him to the Lord for all the days of his life" (1 Samuel 1:11). The passage goes on to say that God granted Hannah's request: She gave birth to a baby boy! It also tells us that Hannah was faithful to the commitment she had made when surrendering her dreams to the Lord Almighty. She took Samuel to the tabernacle and left him there.

Can you imagine taking your three- or four-year-old to church and handing him over to the pastor or priest as an act of surrendering him to God? That's what Hannah did—and the priest had a lousy reputation as a family man! His own sons were immoral and rebellious.

Scripture doesn't say it was easy for Hannah. She was a woman just like you and me. She had agonized in prayer, requesting this child. She had endured mocking from her husband's other wife and the scorn that her culture placed on barren women. After all that, she was willing to part with her deepest desire, sensing that it was in God's will.

Hannah's trust in God was so complete that she was willing to return to Him what she had received from Him. She did not give Samuel to Eli, she gave him to *God*. You see, trust is expressed in surrender to God's will.

Let's also look at the life of Jesus, a son totally submitted to the Father. In John 17:10 Jesus said, "All I have is yours." In Matthew 6:10 He prayed, "Your will be done on earth as it is in heaven." But a test came as He went to Gethsemane and faced His impending death. Like Hannah, He needed to be alone before God. This was not the time for His friends to be offering their opinions concerning the events about to take place. Leaving His disciples behind Him in the garden, He went on and found an altar—a stone—and there He talked to the Father, acknowledging His power. "Father," he said, "everything is possible for you." Then He made His request: "Take this cup from me" (Mark 14:36).

I think there must have been a pause in Jesus' prayer. Maybe an eternity of five or ten minutes. His mind was focused on God, yes, but also on what He knew was ahead.

As I present my wishes to the Lord, I take each three-by-five card one at time and place it loosely in my cupped hands. My wishes and the most precious desires of my heart are open for display. As a physical act of presenting the wish to the

Lord, I extend both arms upward, naming the wish aloud. "Almighty God, I know Your power. Everything is possible with You. I pray that You will see fit to grant this wish." I pour my heart out to my loving heavenly Father.

I linger over each wish, waiting in the Lord's presence, listening to His Spirit speak to mine.

Listening to God's Voice

Though the deep part of us that communicates with God cannot be found by any doctor, it is there. His Spirit speaks to our spirit, we just need to listen.

Gordon MacDonald says that while God's voice is louder than any other sound, it is heard only as we quietly order ourselves to listen. But as with any continuous sound, we find it easy to disregard or even ignore the things we hear, whether the traffic outside or the sound of the furnace at night. Nevertheless, it is impossible to ignore the things we attentively listen for: new parents wait silently to hear the baby's breathing on the first night home from the hospital; a mother watching a church Christmas program can pick her child's voice out of a group recitation or song.

Hannah listened to God's answer to her surrendered wish, and God responded through the voice of Eli. When Hannah's son was a lad under Eli's care, the Lord spoke to him twice in the night. Because he wasn't listening for the Lord, he thought Eli was calling him. Do you remember Eli's response the third time Samuel woke him saying, "Eli, what do you want?" Eli said, "Go and lie down, and if he calls you, say, 'Speak, Lord, for your servant is listening' " (1 Samuel 3:9).

Though the voice of God is rarely audible, He does speak. As Jesus said, the Good Shepherd "Calls his own sheep by name . . . and his sheep follow him because they know his voice" (John 10:3–4).

Nevertheless

In that "eternity" in which Jesus waited in Gethsemane, listening for His Father's response, Jesus heard that there was no acceptable alternative. He knew why He had come to earth and what the Father's plan was. If there were another way, it would have been in place long before He'd come this far. But the plan—that He become human—included taking on this pain and the corresponding human desire to avoid pain. As Jesus realized what He was really asking of the Father, He slowly lifted His head. Blood dripped from His forehead and He said, "Yet not what I will, but what you will" (v. 36b). The King James Version says, "*Nevertheless* not what I will, but what thou wilt."

Nevertheless. I'm so glad Jesus said that. "From my human point of view, I don't want to do this. But from Your heavenly point of view, it must be done. Your ways are best. I will have it Your way."

Just as Jesus was obedient to the Father, we are called to be obedient. Romans 8:29 says, "For those God foreknew he also predestined to be conformed to the likeness of his Son." And Philippians 2:5–8 says:

> Your attitude should be the same
>   as that of Christ Jesus:
> Who, being in very nature God,
>   did not consider equality with God
>   something to be grasped,
>   but made himself nothing,
>   taking the very nature of a servant,
>   being made in human likeness.
> And being found in appearance as a man,
>   he humbled himself
>   and became obedient to death—
>   even death on a cross!

Our attitude to our dreams should carry a *nevertheless*, a desire to be like Jesus—who was obedient.

In his book *The Master's Indwelling*, Andrew Murray perfectly expresses a submissive attitude:

> To my own will I will die; to human wisdom, and human strength, and to the world I will die; for it is in the grave of my Lord that His life has its beginning, and its strength and its glory.

Yes, desiring God's will concerning our wishes and dreams is very demanding. The greater the dreams, the harder the submission. Jesus knew this well when he said, "From everyone who has been given much, much will be demanded; and from the one who has been entrusted with much, much more will be asked" (Luke 12:48).

When I was a teenager at youth camp, it seemed relatively easy to sing, "All to Jesus I surrender, All to Him I freely give." But I didn't have my dreams and heart's desires spread out in front of me then. I didn't have specific hopes for living children and grandchildren with detailed faces and actual names and real personalities. I didn't know how badly I would someday want to have a college education or how much I would want to be thin.

It is one thing to say in general terms, "I want Your will, O Lord," and totally another matter to take a three-by-five card expressing the desire of my heart and surrender it to the Lord.

Here Am I

It is a difficult paradox—in death there is life. As Jesus said, "Whoever wants to save his life will lose it, but whoever loses his life for me will save it" (Luke 9:24). That very principle and paradox is at the core of sanctifying your wishes. Life comes from death.

As you kneel at your altar, lay out your three-by-five cards in a row before the Lord. Slowly read each one. Is this wish more important to you than the life God will give as you consecrate it to God and His wonderful plan for you?

Now, as an act of total surrender, physically sit on the altar with your wishes either in your lap or scattered around you. See yourself as God sees you—a totally surrendered person, a free-will offering, a bride beautiful to her groom.

In *The Master's Indwelling* Andrew Murray says:

> Accept Him in His fullness and let Him teach you how far He can bring you and what He can work in you. Make no conditions or stipulations about failure, but cast yourself

upon—abandon yourself to—this Christ who lived that life of utter surrender to God that He might prepare a new nature which He could impart to you and in which He might make you like himself.

In the quietness of this precious moment, whisper to God your commitment to live in His will, to become what He designed you to become. Look again at each of your wishes. Each one represents not only a request you have of God, but a request He has of you: surrender.

A young man who was struggling to give God all of his life had been advised to let God do the work for him. He said he would try this, and he even cut out letters for a poster which he hung on the wall of his room as a reminder: LET GOD.

In the privacy of his room, he continued to pray; he cried out to God, and finally he just said, "I want to let God have His way, but I can't." In despair he rose from his knees and slammed the door behind him. But when he returned, he was startled to note that slamming the door had loosened a letter on his make-shift poster. With the *D* having fallen to the ground, the motto now read: LET GO.

Throwing himself on his knees beside his bed, he cried, "I will, Lord Jesus. I will."

As you are able to let go of each of your wishes, take a red pen and write diagonally across each card: Nevertheless. "Nevertheless, not my will but thine be done."

Read Galatians 2:20 as your promise that God's ways are better than yours and that His life transforms your death: "I have been crucified with Christ and I no longer live, but Christ lives in me. The life I live in the body, I live by faith in the Son of God, who loved me and gave himself for me."

Knowing God's Will

If you have come this far on your sanctifying journey, God has been speaking to you about your wishes. Spend the rest of the time you have set aside listening to Him. Walk in His creation. Read Scripture. Write down those inner thoughts that the Word nudges in your spirit.

G. Edward Nelson wrote:

> When we get down to basics, the essence of prayer is the bending of our wills into conformity with the will of our Lord. True prayer isn't tinkering with the possibilities of changing God's mind, but is openness to everything He purposes with our lives and for our world. Prayer doesn't alter God; it changes us.

Romans 12 starts with a call to sacrifice and continues with a word about knowing God's will:

> I urge you, brothers, in view of God's mercy, to offer your bodies as living sacrifices, holy and pleasing to God which is your spiritual worship. Do not conform any longer to the pattern of the world, but be transformed by the renewing of your mind. Then you will be able to test and approve what God's will is—his good, pleasing and perfect will.

In one day, God is not likely to tell you exactly

which dreams will be realized. The God who created time makes His will known through time. But as you pray now and throughout the next weeks, God is likely to change some of your priorities. Wishes that were number ones might simply look different under His holy spotlight.

God's Word to you today might be that some of your dreams will die. Let's look at those dreams—the ones to which God may say no—before going on to study God's great *yes!*

CHAPTER FOUR

If Wishes Die

When we submit ourselves as well as our desires to the lordship of Jesus Christ, we are faced with the prospect that some of our wishes and dreams will not become reality. A few may die immediately. More may be pruned to make way for better, stronger dreams.

When you started this book you may have thought that your dreams were dead. But in Part One you discovered that they were only lost or suppressed and could be found and revived. In his book *Why Am I Afraid to Love?*, John Powell says, "When you repress or suppress those things which you don't want to live with, you don't really solve the problem because you don't bury the problem dead—you bury it alive. It remains alive and active inside of you."

When I say that some dreams will die under the shining spotlight of God, I'm not talking about burying them—dead or alive—but releasing them, letting them fly into the hands of the One who holds our future. You bury dreams in anger or disappointment or disillusionment or self-pity, but letting go of something that hinders you frees you to a life of peace, even joy.

Why Some Dreams Die

Why do some of the dreams you wrote out no longer hold their original place in your priorities? When we hold a wish close and private, we do not have an accurate perception of it. We no longer consider the consequences of having it become a reality, nor do we want to. But in the Lord's presence, those same wishes look different.

They Contradict God's Law

If carried out, some wishes would obviously contradict the law and Word of God. You may be in love with someone else's husband and want to run off with him. You may want to get back at someone who did you wrong, and what better way to do it than by planting lies that ruin her reputation? You may desperately wish to keep your own reputation intact—and the only way you can see of doing this is by continuing to lie.

The Word tells us how to deal with these wishes rooted in sin: "Since we are surrounded by such a great cloud of witnesses, let us throw off . . . the sin that so easily entangles, and let us run with perseverance the race marked before us" (Hebrews 12:1).

If you see any wishes that clearly run contrary to God's laws, offer a prayer of repentance and put a big X through the cards as a final symbol of your surrendering them to the Lord. I don't advise throwing cards out, as it's always good to be able to return to your notes.

This release may bring pain. It is easy to think that God is "stripping" us. But in time, it will be clear that God's plans for us are far beyond the plans we have for ourselves that are outside His law. Remember Jeremiah 29:11: " 'For I know the plans I have for you,' declares the Lord, 'plans to prosper you and not to harm you, plans to give you hope and a future.' "

They No Longer Seem Important

Some of our cherished wishes seem unimportant when examined in His sweet presence.

I have always wanted to get a set of Christmas-pattern china. On Christmas Day I'd like my table to look like the ones I see in magazines. But whenever I pray about this desire, it suddenly loses its importance. I already have nice dishes. My table looks lovely, and not just at Christmas.

When the Spirit witnesses with our spirits that a wish, though not evil, is low priority, it can be set aside and periodically reviewed. Actually, the wish is likely to die a natural death as other wishes take on new life.

They Seem Inappropriate

Other wishes may seem inappropriate when brought out in prayer to the Lord. They used to fit, but now they seem the wrong shape.

I once met a man consumed in ministry to the poor of South Korea. When someone sent him a nice coat, he immediately gave it away.

"Why?" I asked him. His coat was worn and obviously needed to be replaced.

"Because," he slowly replied, "it would set me too far above those who have no coat at all."

Though he may have once desired a new garment, the wish was inappropriate, so totally surrendered that it was not even on his mind. The worn coat he had was suitable.

We previously compared wishes to library books. Just as some books eventually become outdated and are no longer useful, some dreams lose their value to us as we change and become more Christlike.

Sometimes God Says "No"

God sometimes says "no," even to dreams that are not based in sin or selfishness. We often think He does this because He's punishing us for some previous sin—and there is some biblical basis for this. Moses dreamed of leading his people across the Jordan River into the Promised Land, but as he approached death he knew he would see the land from afar but never set foot on it (see Deuteronomy 32:48–52). God said this dream was lost because Moses had been unfaithful to Him.

But it's too easy to become preoccupied with our past sins and failures when we try to determine whether or not something is happening because God is punishing us.

More often, if God says "no" to a dream it's because He has a plan that is bigger than ours. Remember the story of Gideon? When God told him that he would defeat the Midianite army, Gideon raised an army of 33,000 men. God simply said, "No, Gideon. Your army is too large. Tell everyone who is afraid of battle to go home." With that, 22,000 men broke rank and left. Then God called for a second troop reduction, which left

Gideon with only 300 soldiers.

You see, it was God's plan to rout the Midianites by frightening them at night with the sound of 300 trumpets blasting and 300 pitchers breaking. God said "no" to Gideon's wish for a large army to make room for another more important wish: victory, the kernel of which He'd already planted within Gideon. When God made it clear that a 33,000-man army was not the way to victory, Gideon put that dream behind him.

Some years ago I had to let a dream die when the Lord showed me that my priorities were not His priorities.

All I wanted was to live in a *finished* house—was that too much to ask? When I was growing up, my dad had worked hard to give us the best he could. But since he had a limited salary and his carpentry skills were used for building other's homes first, we always lived in houses that went on year after year in varying stages of *in*completion. So after Lee and I were married, when my folks offered to sell us their (not completed) home north of St. Paul, even the fact that it was on beautiful Lake Johanna didn't wipe away my negative feelings. At the time, we were in a nice little two-story Victorian with a glassed-in front porch and wall-papered walls. Lee was excited about moving out of the city and living on a lake—and all I could see was that I was returning to something *un*finished! Since Lee was a lab technician and no carpenter, I felt I was returning to some kind of curse I thought I'd escaped.

But we did move in . . . and I hated the house. I hated the unfinished woodwork. I hated the freezing basement. I hated the unfinished front lawn and the mud that tracked in from it with the spring rains (and the summer rains, and the fall rains). I hated the brown kitchen sink and stove, the bathroom with no medicine cabinet, the floors that had never been professionally finished, the fireplace that was unusable, the windows that wouldn't seal right.

For ten years I cried out to God in my personal devotions and prayer time: "I hate this house! Please get me out of here!"

To my delight, Lee's plant finally announced that it would be moving across town. I thought, *This is it! My redemption draweth nigh!* I began to wheedle and make "suggestions" to Lee. Didn't he want to be close to his work?

I persuaded him to at least look at houses. Actually, we looked and looked—but found nothing. I felt so desperate I was ready to move into any bungalow just to get out of that house. Lee, however, was not interested in my short-sighted plan to "run" from an uncomfortable situation.

One thing God gradually made clear to me: My wish for a stable marriage relationship was to be a higher priority than my wish for new scenery! Though my dream of a new house wasn't in itself sinful, it was not to become a reality. Though I cried painful tears of relinquishment, I reestablished my marriage as a top priority and yielded to the leadership of my husband.

But that's not the end of the story. I also made a conscious decision to make that unfinished house into a home. I chose to let that old wish fly away into my Father's loving hands, and I set to work.

Something in me seemed to rise up when I finally accepted things I was powerless to change. If I couldn't change my address, at least I could change my attitude. And I was determined not to live with this hatred.

So I started in, directing my energies toward the hall closet. I worked in a fury, literally closing my eyes and throwing things out of this over-loaded eyesore. I felt as if I were pulling the anger out of my heart. Once I'd sorted, tossed out, and reorganized, I turned on the bathroom closet, the kitchen drawers, the kids closets, and dressers. I really unloaded!

Then I got some paint—a K-mart special! I rifled the sale bins at wallpaper stores. I remade some old drapes into new ones and Lee pitched in to make some new window cornices. Next came a used sofa to match the drapes, and a new coffee table made out of an unusually-shaped piece of wood. Proud of my handiwork, Lee agreed to a new dining room set.

In six months I had transformed the hated house into—if not the home of my dreams—the home I had made my *own*. I had conquered, in more ways than one.

Four years later, we did move—not across town, but across the country. We moved "home" to southern California, my birthplace. We were back in a "nice," finished house, in a neighbor-hood with sidewalks and nice front lawns. But I'd already learned lessons about contentment when His priorities are not mine.

I had learned to rest in the promise of Romans 8:28: "In all things God works for the good of those who love him, who have been called according to his purpose."

When God's "No" Seems Hard

I cannot emphasize enough that we have a God who is trustworthy. Proverbs 3:5–6 says:

> Trust in the Lord with all your heart
>   and lean not on your own understanding;
> in all your ways acknowledge him,
>   and he will make your paths straight.

We don't have a God who sneaks up behind us like some attacker to catch us off guard.

We don't have a Father-God who abandons His children or violates their trust. Jesus is not a friend who turns His back on us when we're needy or in hot water.

I know a woman named Jeannie who was neglected as a little girl. Her mother was a single-parent who had to work full-time—but she also spent most of her free time trying to keep Jeannie's strong-willed older brother out of trouble. Jeannie reached womanhood with the belief that God could provide enough to keep her at subsistence level, but that He was too busy with more important matters to even care about her more sensitive needs. (Can you guess where her ideas came from?)

It's so easy to base our concept of God on our own experiences, rather than on His Word. But God is not simply whomever we imagine Him to be. He has told us who He is in His Word:

God is love. (1 John 4:8)

God is our refuge and strength, an ever present help in trouble. (Psalm 46:1)

Think of the people who have wronged you in the past. Can you say that they can be defined by the one word *love*? The God we can trust is beyond anything we have experienced in our human relationships.

God loves all. The apostles discovered this and told the early believers that God was not only the God of the Jews. "Then Peter began to speak: 'I now realize how true it is that God does not show favoritism'" (Acts 10:34).

God is approachable. "Let us then approach the throne of grace with confidence, so that we may receive mercy and find grace to help us in our time of need" (Hebrews 4:16).

The Christ who died for you and rose again is the only One who can condemn you, and He does not (Romans 8:31–39).

We have a God who is trustworthy because He is love, but also because He knows the future. Can you feel hope surging within you as you consider what it means to have the Almighty God so personally involved in your life—directing your steps into the future? Even when He says no, He is expressing His everlasting, unfathomable love toward us.

But His love does not erase all grief and pain from our lives in this life. Sometimes doing right hurts more than doing wrong. Sometimes letting a wish die hurts—for the moment—more than letting it remain tucked away in a remote corner of the heart, where it festers for years. We saw Jesus agonize in the garden over His impending death. Hebrews 12:2 says that He endured the cross for the joy that was set before Him. You may not feel that joy today, but it will come, as night is followed by morning.

For now, you might simply want to cry. Go ahead and shed those tears of relief, release, and cleansing. This poem by Charles Mackay expresses the importance of our tears:

> O ye tears, O ye tears!
> I am thankful that ye run;
> Though ye trickle in the darkness
> Ye shall glitter in the sun;
> The rainbow cannot shine
> If the rain refuse to fall.
> And the eyes that cannot weep,
> Are the saddest eyes of all.

God welcomes His children's weeping before Him. Nowhere in Scripture did Jesus ever rebuke an individual for crying. Though Scripture never specifically records Jesus' laughing, John 11:35 says "Jesus wept" in sorrow. The apostle Paul confessed that he was a man of tears (Acts 20:19).

As you release your tears in prayer to the Lord, receive the comfort and healing for the grief of wishes and dreams that have died as you have yielded yourself to Him.

"Weeping may remain for a night, but rejoicing comes in the morning" (Psalm 30:5).

That peace and joy will come as you focus on God, not the dead wish. The more I focus on the

Lord, the more I feel the assurance of His guiding hand upon my life.

> You will keep in perfect peace
>   him whose mind is steadfast,
>   because he trusts in you.
> Trust in the Lord forever,
>   for the Lord, the Lord,
>   is the Rock eternal. . . .
> Yes, Lord, walking in the way of your laws,
>   we wait for you;
>   your name and renown
>   are the desire of our hearts.
>   Isaiah 26:3–4, 8

That Lord who is the Rock eternal is the strength we can look to as we walk past our grief and into the future: "My grace is sufficient for you, for my power is made perfect in weakness" (2 Corinthians 12:9).

Rest in the knowledge that God has a future for you beyond that particular wish. As the Lord told His people:

> Forget the former things;
>   do not dwell in the past.
> See, I am doing a new thing!
>   Now it springs up; do you not perceive it?
> I am making a way in the desert
>   and streams in the wasteland.
>   Isaiah 43:18–19

And Jesus said, "I tell you the truth, unless a kernel of wheat falls to the ground and dies, it remains only a single seed. But if it dies, it produces many seeds" (John 12:24).

What a hope that gives us! Hope, such as recorded in the words of this poem:

A gallant heart, defeated,
Now gazing toward the west,
Where this day's splendor crumbles,
Disastrous and unblest—

Look, till the deathlike darkness
By stars be glorified,
Until you see another dream
Beyond the dream that died.

—Author Unknown

When a Wish Won't Die

Before we move on, let me give you a warning: Sometimes a dead dream will come back to life. When we least expect it, when we are focusing on something else—*wham!*—there it is; a wish we thought we'd surrendered is back!

This is especially true when we're tired or discouraged. It can happen when we're feeling hurt or bored. But the return can also be triggered by a simple reminder, an old familiar song or place, a rainy day, or maybe a bright sun. I can't tell you for sure when it will happen, only that it will.

From time to time, painful dreams have tormented me.

One of the wishes I had carried from childhood was this: I wish I could eat whatever I want, whenever I want. With a watchful, caring mother, this wasn't possible until I left home. The consequence of being able to fulfill my wish, however, was that I became terribly overweight and miserable.

In time I totally surrendered that wish to the

Lord. I had surrendered every area of my life to God. I had surrendered self to God. But occasionally that wish would come back. I was especially tempted to eat whenever I had done something great and wonderful, such as vacuuming the carpet, washing the breakfast dishes before going to the office, or getting to the office before 9 A.M. (You know, monumental accomplishments like that!)

The return of that wish to overeat was no gauge of my initial commitment or surrender. No, it simply provided an opportunity for me to learn more about wishes and their realities. You see, there is one very important thing that does *not* happen when you let a wish die.

God Does Not Take Our Wishes From Us

Have you ever prayed, "God take this. I don't want it anymore"? The request doesn't work. Why? Because God doesn't "take," He receives— and only what we surrender.

You can't hold something out to God and expect Him to take it out of your hands. You must lay it on an altar, leave it there, and walk away. Abandon it on the altar and *then* God will do with it as He wills. One man gave his craving for nicotine to the Lord, literally leaving his last pack of cigarettes on a church altar and walking out. For that new Christian, God chose to take away the physical desire for a smoke.

But God isn't one to always work in the same way. In Judges 6, He sent down fire from heaven to consume meat Gideon had offered up to the Lord. What God does with our offering is His business. We only need to leave it on the altar and step away.

If God through His Word has made it perfectly clear that a dream is to die, stand on His Word. Don't be deceived into thinking that because the wish comes back, God is giving you permission to take up a vice! Remember, God tests, but Satan tempts. God tries us, but Satan would torment us. God says, "Obey, then I will show you. Obey, then I will give you." But Satan will show, even display what he will give you. Then, when you give in to him, you have fallen into his trap (see Romans 6:16).

When a sacrificed wish from the past comes back into your mind, think of it as an opportunity to experience a still deeper walk of obedience. It's an opportunity to affirm—not to discount—your sanctifying decision.

Guarding Our Hearts

Proverbs 4:23 says, "Above all else, guard your heart, for it is the wellspring of life." How do you guard your heart? As I surrender dreams that come back to torment, I follow certain steps that you might find helpful.

1. *Openly expose the recurring dream to God's presence.* Pray, "God, I have remembered this wish to _____ . I choose not to hide my thoughts from You. I choose to expose this thought to You. Help me deal with it Your way."

2. *Restate your continued surrender.* Pray, "God, I give You my dream to _____ . As an act of my free will I choose to abandon it by laying it before You as an offering."

3. *Acknowledge this as an opportunity to abandon not only the dream, but self as well.* Tell Him, "Lord, I surrender not only this dream, but I also freely surrender myself to You."

4. *Disown the dream.* In your Dreams Notebook, take a page and draw an altar on it. (You will find a sketch of an old Jewish altar in the reference section of many Bibles.) On top of the sketched altar, draw a box and write the wish inside the box. Write the date on or near the wish and pray, "Father, since I have laid my dream on Your altar, it now belongs to You to do with as You please."

It might be helpful if a trusted friend or counselor prayed with you and for you concerning this commitment. This confidante would not only be there to minister to you with a word of encouragement, she would also serve as a witness to your renunciation. You might want to have this person sign the drawing you made of the dream on the altar. Then reread that page of your notebook whenever you need to be strengthened and encouraged by your decision.

5. *Put yourself totally in God's hands.* He has not forgotten the initial commitment you made to give up this wish. He hasn't forgotten you. He loves you.

Even when you have done this, your dream will still return occasionally. Welcome each recurrence as an opportunity to test your faith and commitment to God's will for your life.

If necessary, read verses such as the following, several times a day until the dream subsides:

Do not be surprised at the painful trial

you are suffering, as though something strange were happening to you. But rejoice that you participate in the sufferings of Christ, so that you may be overjoyed when his glory is revealed. (1 Peter 4:12–13)

Now for a little while you may have had to suffer grief in all kinds of trials. These have come so that your faith—of greater worth than gold, which perishes even though refined by fire—may be proved genuine and may result in praise, glory and honor when Jesus Christ is revealed. (1 Peter 1:6–7)

Consider it pure joy, my brothers, when you face trials of many kinds, because you know that the testing of your faith develops perseverance. Perseverance must finish its work so that you may be mature and complete, not lacking anything. (James 1:2–4)

If the dream persists, there are four more steps you can take to turn this trial into a triumph.

6. *Learn to turn these thoughts into discussions with God.* At this point the real temptation is not in the wish itself as much as in the desire to keep just this one wish independent of God—to start being dishonest with God, thinking you can keep secrets from Him.

7. *Determine to keep every wish exposed to God's Word.* "Your word is a lamp to my feet and a light for my path" (Psalm 119:105). Constant exposure to God's Word is the only sure way to examine all our wishes and dreams; the ones we have determined to let die according to the tugging of the Holy Spirit must be exposed right along with all the rest.

"The word of God is living and active. Sharper than any double-edged sword, it penetrates even to dividing soul and spirit, joints and marrow; it judges the thoughts and attitudes of the heart. Nothing in all creation is hidden from God's sight. Everything is uncovered and laid bare before the eyes of him to whom we must give account" (Hebrews 4:12–13).

During your daily quiet time, record in your notebook scripture passages related to this persistent dream and to obedience, ownership, and commitment.

8. *Claim these specific principles and commands of God's Word.* Reread your notebook and write out relevant verses on small cards or Post-It Notes. Tape or display these where you will see them frequently or at specific times of day when the wish is most regularly on your mind.

With the verses in sight, you can meditate on the principles, not the dream. When the dream persists, quote or read the appropriate scriptures. Choose to think about them instead of the wish.

9. *Be prepared to express your response to each of the specific scriptures.* One form of my journal writing is paraphrasing scripture as it relates to my own needs, including these persistent wishes. I later write some affirmations on cards I keep in my purse. Here are a few that relate to my eating habits:

> I don't eat for reward . . . I have my reward . . . I have holiness and eternal life (see Romans 6:22).

> I trust in the Lord; I choose to do good,

therefore, I dwell in the land and feed on the faithfulness of the Lord. I am truly fed (see Psalm 37:3).

I am learning in my experience what is pleasing to the Lord; I choose to let my life be constant proof of what is most acceptable to Him (see Ephesians 3:18).

I choose not to be vague and thoughtless and foolish, but understanding and firmly grasping what the will of the Lord is. I am constantly filled and stimulated with the Holy Spirit of God (see Ephesians 5:17).

Since I have chosen to place my hope in Christ, I no longer live to eat. I now live for the praise of His glory (see Ephesians 1:12).

I do not surrender to temptations of the flesh, for I am not, nor will I become a slave to the flesh. Rather, I choose to obey God. I choose the way of righteous obedience. Here I am, Father, what would You have me do? (see Romans 6:16).

The only effective way I know to win these painful struggles is to answer them with scripture. Second Corinthians 10:4–5 says:

> The weapons we fight with are not the weapons of the world. On the contrary, they have divine power to demolish strongholds. We demolish arguments and every pretension that sets itself up against the knowledge of God, and we take captive every thought [and dream] to make it obedient to Christ.

When you fight this fight with the weapon of God's Word, you will walk in new strength with victory over that persistent dream.

> How can a young man keep his way pure?
> By living according to your word.
> How does one live according to God's Word?
> I have hidden your word in my heart
> that I might not sin against you.
> Psalm 119:9, 11

When you have God's Word hidden in your heart, and written on cards to keep it before your eyes, you will find the strength to think about other, more profitable things: that which is true, noble, right, pure, lovely, admirable, excellent, and praiseworthy (see Philippians 4:8).

Learn to profit spiritually from these times of testing. Learn to let obedience be your first desire, more precious to you than the persistent wish.

———

Now that you have guarded your heart, will the dream go away? Maybe. And maybe not. But the next time you'll be ready. Don't let its return take you by surprise and distract you from moving on to turn your God-given dreams into realities.

"I press on to take hold of that for which Christ Jesus took hold of me. . . . Forgetting what is behind and straining toward what is ahead, I press on toward the goal" (Philippians 3:12–14).

CHAPTER FIVE

Go, But Slow

The bright side of surrender is that you will discover quite a number of wishes to which God has said *yes*! He didn't give a red light, He gave a green. His word to your heart confirmed that your desire is pleasing to Him. "Let's go," you may be saying.

"Yes, but," is my reply. Do you remember John 10:27, "My sheep listen to my voice; I know them, and they follow me"? As He is the Shepherd, we are the followers. Running ahead of God's timing can be just as disastrous as walking down a path He has marked with a "no."

When God gives the green light, He does not mean for us to "put the pedal to the metal," screeching our wheels even as we get up from our knees after praying. God's green light is something like a flashing yellow. "Go, but proceed with caution." We are not to jump into the intersection, but to follow Him as He goes before us.

Inside so many of us there is still a child, eager to run out ahead of the leader.

A Farmer's Story

Think of your wishes in terms of a farmer's wish for a good crop. He looks out at the fields early one February and sees two feet of snow, caked over with a thin sheet of ice. In his mind he envisions those fields as they were last September, heavy with harvest.

"Lord," he whispers, "please give us a good crop this year."

Within his spirit he recognizes the Lord's voice assuring him of a good harvest. But the experienced farmer knows two things: He must carefully prepare for the harvest, and those preparations must be in season, in tune with God's leading.

Though he doesn't plant seed in February, he may read catalogs then and place his order. He uses this time to service his machinery, making sure it's in good repair and ready for the warmer weather.

The winter may seem like a time of waiting, but that farmer knows that timing is as vital as back-breaking work and sweat. In time he plows and tills the soil. He plants. Even then he takes one step at a time—fertilizing, irrigating, and spraying. Eventually he goes out and cuts the crop—when he knows it's ripe.

It sounds so sensible. Yet how often do we try to jump into the combine, ready to harvest the promised crop even before we till the soil and plant the seed?

Seat Before Feet

Whenever you get off your knees, having heard from God, do not quickly stand and rush out. *Sit* a while and let the Lord give you a glimpse of the plan as well as the promise. Be as eager to listen for instruction as you are to claim the end result. You might remember it this way: "From your knees to your feet by way of your seat."

Isaiah 40:31 says that those who wait on the Lord soar on wings like eagles; they will run and not grow weary, they will walk and not be faint.

I have had many tearful people ask me what went wrong with their dreams. They felt assured of some promise, they stepped out—and everything fell apart.

A number of these people are women who have struggled with weight problems. They've read my book *Free to Be Thin* and they've started an Overeaters Victorious support group in their church. Before they get that group off to a good start (actually, before they've got their own eating problems under control), they set about starting groups all over their city. Soon they're calling me on the phone. They're burned out, gaining weight, and discouraged. What went wrong?

The problem was that they went from their knees to their feet without spending any time reflecting, listening, preparing themselves for what God said was the very next stage of the process that would eventually lead to a harvest. They needed to take the time to get their own problems solved before they offered help to the whole city. A baby learns to creep before learning to walk.

The bigger, the better. The faster, the finer. Right? Not always. You have waited this long, don't rush it now. If God tells you that you will have or be something, that promise is good forever. Waiting one minute or one month for an all-clear, as you lay plans, seek counsel, set goals, and adjust your life to accommodate your wish will not nullify the promise. If God is saying it this morning, He will say it again this afternoon.

Some people say that when God speaks, we are to instantly obey. I disagree. When God speaks, we are to be instantly obedient. That is an attitude of the heart, not necessarily an activity of the feet.

Remember young Samuel's response to the voice of the Lord? "Speak, for your servant is listening" (1 Samuel 3:10). And Mary's? "May it be to me as you have said" (Luke 1:38). Both indicated a willingness to obey, as they were directed.

When God says, "Do," answer Him, "How, Lord?" When He says, "Go," answer, "When, Father?" When God tells you what to do, respond with, "What would You have me do first?" Moving from knees to feet by way of your seat may seem slow motion to some. I see it as self-discipline.

Though some use delay as a subtle way to disobey God, I meet more Christians who run ahead of God than lag behind. Phillips Brooks, the great nineteenth-century preacher, said, "I believe I have spent half my life waiting for God to catch up with me." Does that sound familiar?

Continue to ask these questions, especially in your devotional time as you study God's Word. On your three-by-five cards or in your notebook, write down God's directives to you regarding each dream.

- What biblical character faced a situation similar to the one I face?
- How did that person work it out?
- What are the biblical principles that apply here?
- What biblical principles and references can I hang on to for guidance and affirmation as I walk in obedience?

Silence Before Speech

Though a day will soon come when you should share your dreams with a confidante, move slowly in this regard also. Elizabeth O'Connor gives these wise words:

> In the beginning, we must quietly hover over and protect the nascent or germinating thought until it has toughness and durability. New and emerging ideas that have not been nurtured in their own seed bed should not be spoken of at great length, if at all. They will not survive if they are exposed too early, partly because they are too vulnerable to resist attack or even questioning, and partly because words give them a form and launch them prematurely.

Likewise, Gordon MacDonald reminds us that Jesus lived thirty years in virtual silence before going public with His mission. This silent time is not a passive, wait-and-see time, but purposeful rest for renewal of inner strength, for gaining resolve and clarity to move into the future.

Whenever I take a retreat from my family to identify or sanctify wishes or to determine God's will for the future, upon returning home I first of all allow myself to become reacclimated to my family's world. Experience has taught me that while I have been quietly listening in the presence of the Lord, everybody else has been busy with regular life—and carrying my load as well. When they ask how my retreat has been, I don't immediately pull out my journal and say, "I received a word from God." At first I simply say, "It was great." In time there will be opportunity to share the details.

Reevaluate

As you continue to read His Word and seek His face for direction, reevaluate and prioritize the wishes you have written on your cards. In the lower right corner of each card that is still a viable wish, write new numbers, one being high priority, and five being low priority.

Ask the Lord which few wishes He'd like you to focus on first.

Lord, speak, for Your servant is listening.

PART

THREE

Ratify Your Dreams

*"Let us run with perseverance the race
marked out for us."*
HEBREWS 12:1

CHAPTER SIX

It's Your Move

The things, good Lord, that I pray for, give
me Thy grace to labor for.

—Thomas More

What? Haven't we done all there is to do? Isn't the rest God's responsibility? Can't we just remind Him from time to time that He is supposed to be taking the lead in making our dreams come true?

Doesn't Psalm 37:5 (KJV) say, "Commit thy way unto the Lord; trust also in him; and he shall bring it to pass"? Since childhood I've heard, "Give it to God and He will do it." (Just what I was to give was unclear, and what He would do was equally unclear.) The inference was that I had no responsibility other than "giving," and He had all the responsibility of "doing." Interpreted this way, the verse became a coupon to be redeemed at will—my will.

Then does this mean everything that happens in my life is from an *external force,* rather than an *internal strength?* Is God "waiting on high" to do whatever we ask, waiting to hear our petitions, which He is then obligated to fulfill?

The verb *commit* appears again and again in the Scriptures: "Commit to the Lord whatever you do, and your plans will succeed" (Proverbs 16:3). Does this mean that if we've told God our dreams and verbally made Him our partner, He will automatically make sure everything happens in our favor?

And 2 Chronicles 16:9 says, "For the eyes of the Lord range throughout the earth to strengthen those whose hearts are fully committed to him." Does this mean that if I give Him my heart, He must give me the strength to do whatever I want? ("Hey, God. Here I am. Yoo-hoo, over here!")

I've also known people who have lived a Christian version of *que sera, sera,* "what will be will be." "I will just concentrate on being totally God's, and whatever happens, happens."

In 1 Kings 8:61, we find a more complete picture of what our commitment to God involves: "But your hearts must be fully committed to the Lord our God, to live by his decrees and obey his commands." Our commitment to God must include commitment to His ways. Our commitment involves our wills and our work. We must follow the Lord's leading, but we are also responsible for putting one foot in front of the other. While we should move from our knees to our feet by way of our seat, it's a mistake to stay there!

For our dreams to become reality, we must not only identify and sanctify them; we must also ratify them. For our purposes, let's define *ratify* as the actions we must take to make our wishes and dreams our own.

Taking Responsibility

Let me quote again Hebrews 12:1: "Therefore, since we are surrounded by such a great cloud of witnesses, let us throw off everything that hinders and the sin that so easily entangles, and let us run with perseverance the race marked out for us."

I usually hear this scripture taught in regard to the importance of Christian living and standards we must hold to. I see that concept in this verse, but I also see another lesson: Who is to throw everything off and run the race? *We* are. Our wishes call us to take personal responsibility.

God is not a "fairy godmother" who waves a magic wand over our wishes—even if they have been implanted by Him and are meant to bring us into the fullest life He has for us. Of course God has the power to speak our requests into being (after all He spoke the universe into being), but under such a system we would never stretch into maturity. Parents happily wait on a week-old baby hand and foot. But there's something tragic about a six-year-old child who cannot feed herself—maturity has been stunted. Responsibility comes with maturity.

When I was very young, Grandma Sampson always had a hanky in her pocket. When the need arose, she would wipe my nose for me. But then the day came when she said to me, "Neva, go get a Kleenex and wipe your nose." She knew that the time had come for me to take responsibility for this aspect of my personal hygiene. No one would doubt that it was the loving thing for her to do. She wasn't going to follow me around for the rest of my life, hanky in hand!

Just as we can't expect God to bring our wishes to completion for us, so we can't expect loved ones to do it either. In her book *The Cinderella Complex*, Colette Dowling describes the all-too-traditional woman who "wants to be taken care of in preference to being responsible and productive."

When we all get to heaven, God will not say to your husband, "What did you do with the dreams I gave your wife?" A husband will be held accountable by God as to how he encouraged or discouraged the gifts and callings and dreams God gave to his wife (see Ephesians 5:25–29), whether or not he loved her as himself, and whether or not he fed and cared for her emotions and spirit. But you and I will be held accountable concerning our own gifts and their development. None of us will be able to make our spouse an alibi or excuse.

Regardless of the support (or the lack of it) you receive from those closest to you, it is God who calls and gifts you—and God who will carry you through.

Are You Ready for Commitment?

Often our wishes don't become reality for the simple reason that we aren't committed to work for them. Commitment may start at an altar of prayer, but it is worked out in daily living. Being committed involves being determined to carry out a course of action. It moves our wishes from the impossible or improbable realm of "what if" or "I could" into the possible realm of "with God's help, I will."

Think of the story of the Prodigal Son, a destitute young man tending pigs and so hungry that he's eating their feed. He's previously left a kind and wealthy father whom he has disappointed. His *what if*'s and *I could*'s might have looked like this:

What if Father heard about my situation?

What if a relative sees me here?

What if a kind person were to come and offer me help to get out of here?

What if I were to go home?

What if I got a better job?

But Luke's gospel account says that the young man stepped above the *what if*'s and *I could*'s and went to the *I will*'s:

"I will set out and go . . ." (Luke 15:18).

In *Vital Signs*, George Barna and William Paul McKay perceptively comment that "commitment implies motivation, and it appears that this is where the system breaks down for Christians. Many born-again people want faith to be easy."

Does their analysis sound familiar? How badly do you want your dreams to come true?

But I'm Afraid

Commitment is a frightening word. What if we fail not only ourselves but *God*? But Jesus told an interesting parable that is really about this fear of risk. A man going on a journey called together his servants and entrusted talents to each. One received five, one received two, and the third man received one. The first two servants put their money to work and doubled their investment. The third, afraid of the risk of any investment, chose safety. He buried his talent in the ground and simply waited for the day when the master would return.

Well, eventually the master did return—full of praise for the servants who had gone out and invested, but full of fury at the man whose excuse was "I was afraid" (Matthew 25:25). The master described the fear in other terms: "You wicked, lazy servant. . . . You should have put my money on deposit with the bankers, so that when I returned I would have received it back with interest" (vv. 26–27).

God's Commitment to Us

This parable of the talents makes another point about commitment: It is not simply a one-way street. Where does the story start? With a master who committed talents into the care of stewards. I challenge you with this thought: The wishes and dreams that you still have after going through the exercises in this book are dreams that God has entrusted to you. God committed your dreams to you before you committed them to Him. His great plans for you predated your dreams for yourself!

Paul recognized that commitment is a two-way transaction when he said to Timothy, "And of this gospel I was appointed a herald and an apostle and a teacher" (2 Timothy 1:11). Paul, who had committed his life and ministry to God, also realized that God had committed the ministry to him, asking him to be responsible for "investing," not "hiding," the "dream."

Stop for a second and meditate on this wonderful thought: *Your dreams can show you God's path to becoming what and whom He has designed you to be.* As you commit yourself to God and to your dream, you *are* committing yourself to becoming whom He designed you to be. And all the while you're becoming whom and what you want to be!

Making a commitment to a specific dream can be hard. Elizabeth O'Connor referred to this in her book *The Eighth Day of Creation*:

> I would rather be committed to God in the abstract than to be committed to Him at the point of my gifts. When one really becomes practical about gifts, they spell out responsibility and sacrifice. Commitment at the point of my gifts means that I must give up being a straddler. My commitment will give me an identity.

Without that commitment to a dream, we deny ourselves the joy of discovering whom we were meant to be—our very identities.

We started this chapter by looking at Psalm 37:5. Let's read it again in a larger context: "Commit your way to the Lord; trust in him and he will do this:" The colon indicates something to follow and gives meaning to the preceding phrases. What will the Lord do? Verse 6 says, "He will make your righteousness shine like the dawn, the justice of your cause like the noonday sun."

"He will make . . ." immediately reminds me of Jesus' words to His disciples: "Come, follow me, and I will make you fishers of men" (Matthew 4:19).

In Psalm 37:5, the word *make* refers to a change in the deepest part of a person. In Matthew 4:19, the word *make* also refers to a dramatic change from what was before. As we commit ourselves to God and to our dreams, God does a work deep within us, molding us into His design—not by external force but by internal change.

Jesus is saying, "Come, follow Me. Commit your way to Me, and by a work I will do deep within you, you shall become something you were not before."

Where to Start?

You may still be saying, "But what if I commit myself to my dream and fall flat on my face?" The question is answered only as we commit ourselves to being faithful to our dream rather than to the success of our dream. In the parable of the talents the master expected the servant to invest the talent entrusted him; the master did not expect the servant to rig the bank's interest rates. We must give permission to possibility.

Several years ago a Christian ministry had a slogan: "How do you eat an elephant? One bite at a time." Making a commitment to work toward your grand dreams is possible only as you commit yourself to taking small steps—goals that serve as guideposts, showing you how far you've traveled on your journey.

If You Never Start the Race, You Never Finish It!

As I was researching this book, I asked fifty Christians if they ever set goals. Forty-five answered "yes." But only two said that they always met the goals they set. At first I was alarmed. *Are we such an undirected people?* I wondered. But the more I thought about it, the more comforted I was by these statistics. Why? Because I knew I would be in the group that sets goals they never reach.

Why is that where I stand? Because I set some goals high enough to keep me stretching. I had one goal that seemed unreachably high to me—to learn to use the computer on which I'm writing this book. Though the task was monumental, I outdid myself and have mastered it.

I, for one, would rather set goals I never meet than never set goals at all. You see, as a Christian I am a "prisoner of hope" (Zechariah 9:12). We have not only the hope of eternal life; the energizing power and life of the Holy Spirit within us gives us hope for this life.

Will you make the decision to become a reality thinker instead of a wishful thinker?

CHAPTER SEVEN

Going for the Gold

Don't let your wishes die of neglect. Keep them alive with goals.

"Wishes *can* become true," promises a Sears Financial Network brochure. It goes on to say, "A secure home, a sound financial future . . . Wishing and hoping and thinking and dreaming won't bring your goals any closer, but planning for them will."

The Bible says it a little differently:

> Set up road signs;
>   put up guideposts.
> Take note of the highway,
>   the road that you take.
> Jeremiah 31:21

What Is a Goal?

If we see our wishes become reality, it will not be by accident. It's not likely to be because we were in the right place at the right time or because we return a lucky sweepstakes entry. It is likely to be because we, in faith, planned for our wishes to become reality, and smart planning calls for the setting of specific goals.

Think about goals in terms of a sports event. A runner stays a narrow course, heading for a ribbon that marks the finish line. The front line of a soccer team expends all its energy to get the ball into the goal.

In planning for our own future, goals are specific *marks* toward which we "run" if we are to see the fulfillment of a wish. The identified desires of our heart can be defined as our long-term goals. But specific intermediate steps are necessary for us to see how we can get to that grand, seemingly unreachable goal.

Imagine a team of first-grade soccer players eagerly playing the first game of their lifetime. A friend recently told me that she'd watched such a game from the sidelines. The kids knew that their wish was to win the game. But they hadn't been given more than ten minutes of pre-game instruction. In the excitement of the hour and in their growing fatigue, mayhem broke out. Children kicked the ball toward the wrong goal. Some stared off into space, forgetting that they were to pay attention to the ball. The long-term goal of winning the game got lost for lack of short-term, immediate goals that first graders could think about.

As budgets are ideas expressed in dollars, faith is dreams expressed in setting and working toward goals. "Faith by itself, if it is not accompanied by action, is dead," says James 2:17.

Why Set Goals?

Goals Give Clear Direction and Sharpen Our Focus

This is especially true of long-terms goals that identify our desired eventual destination. Some people move through life as if they were headed from Los Angeles to New York City with a map that is only an outline of the U.S. Their map doesn't indicate where either city is or where the roads are. At every single intersection these people struggle in deep prayer, looking for divine guidance for their decision.

"Where are you going?" you might ask them.

"To New York City," they answer confidently.

"How will you get there?"

"God will show us along the way," they respond.

Later they wonder how they arrived in Maine. "Oh well, it must have been the Lord's will," they surmise.

But along the way they didn't even look for the obvious signs that showed them they were off course. The sun always rises in the east, providing direction for the wayward traveler, yet in their distraction they didn't notice that they were always driving north.

Proverbs 4:25 says it this way: "Let your eyes look straight ahead, fix your gaze directly before you."

Goals Help You Plan Your Course

In our hypothetical trip from Los Angeles to New York, we can choose one of many routes.

Should we drive through the Northern states or stay in the South? And how should we get there? If our primary interest is in getting there fast, perhaps we should buy a nonstop airline ticket. But if we want to see the country, maybe we should travel by train. If we want to be able to stop frequently to sightsee and look at anything that catches our interest, we probably should drive.

Proverbs 4:26 says, "Make level paths for your feet and take only ways that are firm."

The "firm" way often is a course between two extremes. On one hand, a course that is too easy requires no faith or courage on our part; but we know that some fear is healthy. In *The Strong and the Weak*, Paul Tournier notes, "No endeavor is fruitful without fear. There is no good actor who does not have to contend with stage fright."

On the other hand, choosing the most dangerous possible course is probably foolish and potentially disastrous. Setting realistic goals helps us to discover the responsible and possible way to make our wishes become reality.

For example, as I've pursued my college degree, I've learned that I want and need to take a "sightseer's drive across the country." I enjoy experimenting; so when my children were little, I took correspondence courses. I've taken extension classes from the university and courses at the local community college. On the side, to meet my broader wish of furthering my education, I attend conferences and seminars. (I've discovered that the joy is not only in arriving, but in the route I take to get there!)

How to Set Goals

When we set goals we are defining a realistic plan of action that takes into consideration our deadlines and time frames, resources, costs, support systems, and current responsibilities. I have had to plan my educational pursuits by keeping in mind my family responsibilities, work load, financial resources, and emotional needs. Fortunately they all fit together.

As you look over your wishes, choose several for which you want to write out specific goals. In Chapter 2, I suggested that you categorize your wishes into life areas: family life, spiritual life, vocation, Christian ministry, hobbies, physical health, emotional health, social relationships, finances, and education. For this exercise you might feel led to choose wishes from differing categories.

At the end of the book I've included several worksheets you might want to photocopy as you set goals in several of these life areas.

Time Frame

Goals are most effective for keeping us on course if they are articulated with a specific time frame so we can measure our results. The time frame might look like this:

If I want to _____ in five years, then this year I must _____ , this month I need to _____ , and this week I must _____ , so today I will _____ .

A neighbor had lived in her house ten years

without giving it a thorough, top-to-bottom clean-ing. She set a goal to thoroughly clean her house within a year. To accomplish her larger goal, she set smaller goals. She'd clean the closets first, then the kitchen cupboards. Having short-term goals served the purpose of keeping her focused. She didn't have to worry about the kitchen cupboards while she was cleaning the closets because she knew they were next on her list. She had small victories to celebrate whenever one task was fin-ished.

What Will It Cost?

The decisions we make (or don't make) always seem to come with a price tag. You might say life is a balance sheet—full of debits and credits.

I love what Elizabeth O'Connor said on this point in *The Eighth Day of Creation*: "When we choose to leave our house and prisons of protec-tion to stand in the warm light of the sun, we will suddenly someday be aware it is also the place where the wind blows." She realized that there are costs, trade-offs, involved in stepping out.

The price we will have to pay to meet a goal can often be calculated in advance. Jesus himself understood this in a teaching on the cost of dis-cipleship: "Suppose one of you wants to build a tower. Will he not first sit down and estimate the cost to see if he has enough money to complete it?" (Luke 14:28).

As you set goals, the obvious answer to this question of cost can sometimes be calculated in dollars and cents. If your dream is to go to grad-uate school, how many hours do you need to take, at what cost per hour? How much does the school estimate that books and other expenses will be? You'll have to add in room and board or commuting costs.

But there are other costs. How much time will reaching your goal require of you? How much energy? Will the meeting of your personal goals cost your family something? What? If you're going to reach goal #1, will something else have to become a lower priority?

Each of these measurable or unmeasurable costs should be calculated into your original goals.

A few years ago, Lee and I made a specific financial goal: to pay off our thirty-year mortgage in fifteen years. This goal was one way to work toward the larger dream of greater financial independence.

To set our mortgage goal, we did some homework and we counted the cost. From a bank we secured an amortization schedule and discovered that the goal was much more manageable than we had originally anticipated. If we reduced certain controllable expenses and paid the mortgage holder just a few more dollars each month, we could reach our goal!

As you may know, most of that humongous mortgage payment is *interest*. By making arrangements to pay each month's regular bill plus the next month's principal payment, we set—and have held to—a goal that gets us toward the larger wish.

I have also had to count the cost as I've set— and tried to keep—my goal of exercising for a period of time each day. This is a specific goal I've set to help me reach my larger goal of being physically fit. I know the value of exercise. When I do it, I have fewer headaches and feel less tense, yet actually setting my body in active motion is very hard for me.

I have taken time to figure out the problems: When I get up in the morning I would much rather read or write than exercise. But if I leave it to the end of the day, family responsibilities and my own tiredness override my discipline. Then it's too easy to say that I'll put it off until the morning.

In figuring out the costs involved in meeting this goal, I looked at my options. Do I *have* to read first thing in the morning? No. I'm so naturally motivated to read that I can do it anytime of the day, even in short spurts, and still receive maximum benefit. Do I *have* to write first thing in the morning? No. I can shut the door to my office and write for hours each day after breakfast without interruption. My creativity doesn't die if I don't get an idea down when I first wake up.

Do I *have* to exercise first thing in the morning? Yes. If I don't do it then, I don't do it at all. The cost of being physically fit is getting up thirty minutes earlier in the morning and getting my feet in motion.

From Paper to Progress

Written goals are great, but once again, it's working toward goals that makes wishes become reality. On paper I can have grand designs of exactly what I have to do today and next week and next month to meet a certain goal in five years.

I could have planned out that college degree in ten different schedules, but if I'd never taken aptitude tests to see what areas my personality and abilities best suited, sent for catalogs, applied for courses at schools that accommodated my learning style and interests, registered, and shown up for class, my goals would have profited me nothing. As James might say: "A goal without corresponding works is dead" (James 2:26).

When she was in her forties, Hulda Crooks decided she wanted to see a dream to be a mountain climber come true. She knew that meant she had to start exercising. Only she could translate her commitment to get and stay in shape from paper to progress. And do you know the end of the story? At age ninety-three she climbed Mount Fuji!

Now I've seen Mount Fuji—from the air and from the ground at some distance. It's some mountain. While most grandmothers would have been lounging, feeling that they deserved to retire after their years of labor, a committed Hulda worked to plant her feet on top of that mountain—because she was willing to say "I will."

"Do you not know that in a race all the runners run, but only one gets the prize? Run in such a way as to get the prize" (1 Corinthians 9:24).

In your Dreams Notebook keep track of the progress you make toward each of your goals. Set aside a few pages for each of the wishes you've chosen to work on. Write the goal at the top of the page. Each morning make a diary-type entry, writing down what you intend to do that day to meet your next short-term goal in that area. The next morning read the previous day's entry and place a "V" for Victory in the margin if you complete the assignment.

A Word About Accountability

A discussion of goals isn't complete without mention of accountability. In our society woven with the fabric of individualism and independence, *accountability* seems like a foreign word.

In Christian circles, I see two extremes: Some people resist being accountable to anything and anyone—even God it seems. Others have gone overboard, giving up even simple individual decision-making so that they do nothing if someone has not told them exactly what to do. But a balanced view and practice of accountability is normal and natural. In one sense it's what setting goals is all about. Even self-driven goals give us a structure for accountability.

As Gordon MacDonald says in *Ordering Your Private World*, "If my private world is in order, it will be because I see myself as Christ's steward and not as master of my purpose, my role, and my identity."

Stewardship assumes accountability, first and foremost to God's revealed will in the Bible. Jehoshaphat said, "First seek the counsel of the Lord" (1 Kings 22:5). The goals you set and the road to reaching them must always line up with the teachings of Scripture. A "nudge" that doesn't align with His Word can be discounted. Psalm 32:8–9 gives both a promise for guidance and a charge to be guidable:

> I will instruct you and teach you in the
> way you should go;
> I will counsel you and watch over you.
> Do not be like the horse or the mule,
> which have no understanding but must
> be controlled by bit and bridle or they will
> not come to you.

Being accountable also involves a trusted relationship with one or more persons who can help keep us on the right road. Proverbs 15:22 says, "Plans fail for lack of counsel, but with many advisers they succeed."

Why are these people important? They give us a fresh perspective on our dreams and goals. When we can't see the forest for the trees, they help us see the big picture. When we get bogged down, they remind us of how far we've come. They help us anticipate the victories ahead.

I couldn't do without my close friends Judy, Marieta, Janet, and Pat. Each of them recognizes my need to maintain a certain level of interdependence and puts my needs and interests on par with her own. Each of them helps me anticipate problems and explore solutions.

Being accountable to another person or persons does not involve running out and baring your soul to everyone you see. ("May I tell you my precious dreams? Here, these are the costs I expect to incur. This is the scriptural encouragement I've discovered. . . . What do you think?")

Let me warn you, not everyone is ready to hear your story. Not everyone deserves your trust. And a few will think it their place to "talk some sense" into your head about your foolish notions. Some people make a career out of doubt and negative thinking; they are dream killers who think they are doing you a favor by forcing you to consider your dream from all angles.

For counsel and accountability choose an objective and trusted person—possibly your pastor, a trusted friend, a Christian counselor, or your mate. Look for someone who is actively pursuing goals of his or her own, who takes responsible risks, who exemplifies a firm faith and a willingness to work hard. "Sniff out" this kind of positive person, maybe in a Sunday school class or Bible study group. Make friends and explore the idea of being accountable to each other.

We all encounter enough rebuke in our lives that we don't need to go looking for more. Seek out a mentor who knows how to confront and guide without having a critical spirit.

One day I opened my mail and read an ad for the *Writer's Digest* School for Writers: "You've dreamed about it long enough. . . . Open the door to the writer's life *now*." The next paragraph described the program and gave a description of a good relationship of accountability:

> You will have . . . a professional writer almost looking over your shoulder as you write. . . . Your instructor will build on your strong points, correct your weaknesses, and help you develop your personal writing style. . . . Your instructor will remain with you . . . counseling and encouraging you. . . .

The writing instructor doesn't actually complete the work for you; you are responsible for the product, but that person provides correction, counsel, and encouragement. A good mentor is interested in your progress—not in your failure. She doesn't push you too hard, but nudges you to be and do your best. She doesn't heap you with guilt or violate your person. Ecclesiastes 4:10 summarizes this partnership:

> If one falls down,
> his friend can help him up.
> But pity the man who falls
> and has no one to help him up!

Through experience and from talking to others I see the wisdom in sharing one's dreams and goals gradually, especially if a relationship is new. You've had an entire lifetime to think about your dreams and desires, but a confidante needs time to get to know you bit by bit. Your goals need time to solidify in your mind and heart.

As your relationship grows, experiment with three kinds of goals: those you set for yourself and for which you look to your mentor for encouragement and accountability; those your mentor suggests to you; and imposed goals that your mentor (say, an editor, aerobics instructor, or tutor) gives you as a condition of continuing the accountability relationship.

The Big Picture

As you set and start to work on short-term goals, always keep the big picture in mind. Are your goals helping you make your dreams come true? Are they helping you serve the cause of

Christ, or are they ultimately distracting you from the *big picture*? In *Making It Happen*, Charles Paul Conn says, "Looking through a peephole is no way to stay motivated when you're moving toward a goal. The big view is important."

There have been days when I've gotten so bogged down writing a chapter or section of a book that I've nearly lost sight of the hope of finishing the manuscript.

Whenever I list my goals, I write this verse at the top of the sheet: "So we make it our goal to please him" (2 Corinthians 5:9). This is my number one goal to which all others must submit. And with that as my ultimate goal I'm continually reminded to turn to Him for strength and guidance. Galatians 3:3 gives this admonition: "Are you so foolish? After beginning with the Spirit, are you now trying to attain your goal by human effort?"

Yes, we should pursue goals with determination and decisive action—but not stubbornly. In setting and working toward goals, keep in mind that they should be firm without being rigid. They are valuable as long as they are helping you move toward your ultimate God-entrusted dreams.

If, in time, you see that your goals are taking you in a wrong or unwise direction, don't panic and quickly desert the original wish. Take time to listen to God's Word, to reevaluate. The "mistake" may well be the short-term goal, not the original dream.

Remember the small goal is not important apart from the God-given "yes" you're headed toward.

CHAPTER EIGHT

Facing Obstacles

I am always challenged when I read two or more scripture verses that seem to contradict one another. Two such verses are Proverbs 3:6, "In all your ways acknowledge him, and he will make your paths straight," and 2 Timothy 4:7, "I have fought the good fight, I have finished the race, I have kept the faith."

Is it possible that these two verses, one seemingly full of the promise to make everything easy and the other a statement by Paul that life has been a fight, aren't contradictory but supportive of each other?

I believe so. *Strong's Exhaustive Concordance* says when the Bible speaks of the path or way being straight, it does not mean that it is made *easy*, but rather *plain*. To me that speaks of direction and decisions.

While decisions may be made clear, at times the way may be tough-going. So we can identify our dreams and finally see what we were designed to be, but getting there may take work and, occasionally, even extreme effort on our part. Setting goals without expecting obstacles guarantees disappointment, discouragement, and failure.

What Is an Obstacle?

Simply, an obstacle is anything that gets in the way. The dictionary refers to obstacles as barriers, deterrents, hindrances, hurdles, impediments, restraints, and difficulties.

Being a Christian does not exempt you from encountering obstacles. They're part of the human experience. Jesus said, "He causes his sun to rise on the evil and the good, and sends rain on the righteous and the unrighteous" (Matthew 5:45).

Job 14:1 makes this clear statement concerning human life: "Man born of woman is of few days and full of trouble." Job's life is a reminder that obstacles blocking our paths do not necessarily mean that we are out of God's will.

But the Bible makes one thing clear about obstacles: They cannot separate us from Christ's love:

> For I am convinced that neither death nor life, neither angels nor demons, neither the present nor the future, nor any powers, neither height nor depth, nor anything else in all creation, will be able to separate us from the love of God that is in Christ Jesus our Lord. (Romans 8:38–39)

Why Obstacles?

C. H. Spurgeon said, "The Lord gets His best soldiers out of the highlands of affliction." Hebrews 5:8 says that Jesus "learned obedience from what he suffered," and Romans 5:3–5 refers to obstacles saying that:

... suffering produces perseverance; perseverance, character; and character, hope. And hope does not disappoint us, because God has poured out his love into our hearts by the Holy Spirit, whom he has given us.

Let me quote C. H. Spurgeon again:

Delayed answers to prayer are not only trials of faith, but they give us opportunities of honoring God by our steadfast confidence in Him under apparent repulses.

Obstacles Make Overcomers

As I read accounts of overcomers in the Bible, I'm reminded of a great truth: Obstacles make overcomers. Though you can have obstacles without being an overcomer, you can't be an overcomer without having obstacles to overcome.

Think of Naomi, who buried her husband and then her two sons. Her loss was not only her family; buried with them were her present and her hope for a future livelihood. Her obstacles were monumental: She was living in a foreign land, poor and alone with two foreign daughters-in-law. Naomi, whose name means "pleasantness, my joy," asked God to change her name to Mara, meaning "bitterness," because she felt God had dealt bitterly with her.

Despite her depression, Naomi started to make plans to return to the Land of Promise, to her own people. When daughter-in-law Ruth insisted that she go along with Naomi, this complicated Naomi's plan. Though she no longer had to travel alone, she now had to face her people with—and provide for—Ruth, a foreigner. One obstacle replaced another.

Naomi and Ruth's story is an account of the two women overcoming one obstacle after another. But in the end, Naomi's wish for a secure future and a grandchild was realized, as Naomi successfully coached Ruth on how to "catch" Boaz for her husband.

The book of Judges relates an account of Deborah, a woman who faced different obstacles, the details of which we can only speculate about. We do know that she was a woman doing what was considered by most to be a man's job. She was married and worked outside of the home, in a time and culture that dictated a woman rarely leave her home. She also owned land in a time when women did not hold title to property. And she presided over court even though women were not even permitted to give testimony in court.

Attitudes as Obstacles?

Can you imagine the obstacles Deborah had to overcome in facing the attitudes of the men and women of her day?

In his book *Making It Happen*, Charles Paul Conn notes that attitudes are often the obstacles that we have to overcome to meet our goals:

> Achievement of great goals must always occur in the face of misunderstanding and often outright criticism. . . . Winston Churchill was disgraced by the failures of British naval policy during World War I and was so devastated by critics that he was gen-

erally thought to be finished as a career politician. But he came back, at the age of sixty-six, to become Prime Minister of England and carve his mark as one of the greatest leaders of this century.

I've faced some of these obstacles as I've been pursuing several of my wishes.

When I'm faced with an obstacle of any sort, I can choose to see it as a reason to quit or as a challenge to continue to seek God and His righteousness and persevere on the path He sets before me.

Unforeseen Obstacles

Many obstacles we encounter as we work toward our goals will be foreseen. We might identify them in terms of the costs of meeting goals. But some obstacles will take us by surprise and make us feel helpless in our pursuit. Many of these obstacles are other people—who have wills of their own. When personalities or committees make decisions that affect us seemingly adversely, we can only do so much to try to change the situation. Ultimately we cannot force another person to change, to see the world as we see it.

I ran into one such obstacle as I was working toward ordination. To meet this long-term goal, my short-term goals were prescribed for me. I had to—and did—meet very specific educational requirements. But then the denomination changed its policy: Only those who planned to be involved in specific preaching or pastoral ministries could be ordained.

Since this was neither my call nor my goal, the officials explained to me their alternate option: I could receive a license in specialized ministry. At this point I had to reevaluate my goals in terms of the big picture. Was ordination so important to me that I would change denominations or apply for "papers" from a less than reputable "ordination mill"?

I was disappointed. I have been encouraged to apply for change in status. However, I have chosen to accept the Specialized License. It does not change what I do, nor does it change how I feel about what I do. I have chosen to be content with this, especially since I do not serve on a church staff. In some cases it even works in my favor.

Usually, I do not even mention that I am a "Reverend"—except to my children when I try to use it to my advantage.

A Mother's Pain

Some time ago I was faced with another obstacle that caused me much more pain than the postponement of ordination. What is more dear to a mother's heart than her daughter? When it came to my relationship with my younger daughter, my dream of being a good mother seemed out of reach. How I identify with the father in the parable of the Prodigal Son!

Several years of household stress and tension, yelling, screaming, and tearful pleading abruptly ended when our seventeen-year-old daughter moved out of the house. Since before her sixteenth birthday, she had refused to let me touch her. Normal conversation had ceased; we had either yelled at each other or not spoken at all. Most of the time my relationship with her had left me feeling panicked.

Finally, someone let me know they'd seen her in a compromising situation in full daylight in a parking lot outside the school she was attending. All this happened at a time when she was already grounded and was not supposed to be seeing her boyfriend at all.

When we had our confrontation over the issue, I told her she must either live by our standards of conduct or choose to live elsewhere. I could not take any more emotional battering. After only a few seconds' thought, she shrugged and said, "Fine. I'll move out."

That was the moment I gave up. All my dreams of being the ideal Christian mother to this child seemed to blow away like smoke in the wind. I called her boyfriend and asked him to come and take her to where she was going. Then I walked to her room feeling totally numb, and I helped her pack.

When her boyfriend's truck pulled out of our driveway, carrying my daughter away from me, three years of pain and rejection burned within my chest and finally exploded in sobs. In terrible pain, I collapsed. Sobs came that I hardly recognized as human. I cried so hard that my rib cage was sore for several days afterward. Somehow I had failed this child, failed God as a Christian mother. What had I done to ruin our relationship?

The following days were awful, as I had no

idea of where she was. She had no money; how would she survive? What would she eat? Where would she sleep? I contacted her school counselor, who played intermediary so I could get an address to get in touch with her. But the days turned to weeks and we didn't hear from her.

One day I tried to pray for her and couldn't. The pain of even praying seemed more than I could bear. For months I couldn't pray. I could only feel pain, which I tried to stuff deep within myself as I went about my daily activities.

But then came Christmas. I bought her presents and put them under the tree. I waited. I hoped, and finally when I took the tree down I put the gifts in a closet. The physical pain I felt between my ribs took my breath away, and that day I fell in total brokenness and surrender before God. I laid before Him my petitions and my pain. Again I sobbed, this time not in anger but in release. I put both my daughter and myself— my pain—on the altar: *Lord, I release her to You.* In the words of Job, I prayed, "The Lord gave and the Lord has taken away; may the name of the Lord be praised" (Job 1:21). *Lord, I give You my desire to have her in my life. Please replace my pain with Your peace.*

That day the heaviness lifted; for the first time in over a year I felt a peace that was beyond my understanding. It came as I gained new understanding of Philippians 4:6–7:

> Do not be anxious about anything, but in everything, by prayer and petition, with thanksgiving, present your requests to God. And the peace of God, which transcends all

understanding, will guard your hearts and your minds in Christ Jesus.

I can't say that I prayed with much thanksgiving. I prayed with pain, but when the peace came, thanksgiving flooded me.

Spring came and graduation approached. I went to the school counselor and, feeling like a beggar, asked for tickets to the ceremony. (My daughter had given away all her tickets to her boyfriend's family and other friends.)

As the gowned graduates walked down the aisle, Lee and I scanned the faces. There she was! I took pictures like every other proud parent. No one would have suspected that my daughter and I hadn't spoken for over a year and a half; no one would have suspected that my tears were anything other than normal motherly tears.

I had run out of all but faith. Reuben Welch has a book titled *When You Run Out of Fantastic, Persevere.* That title tells the story of my life during those months.

In the next few weeks I realized that the faith that was growing in me was stronger than any pain I felt. God was asking me to give Him time, to wait for reconciliation. The faith the Lord was asking of me required that I persevere in patience, not that I step forward in faith. I can hear the accusers: "You call this faith? Admit it. You say you are waiting and resting, but really you have given up." Have you ever been tempted to harass others into seeing a situation your way when the wiser course of action would have been to simply voice an opinion and let God work His ways in His time?

It is easier to think of faith as an activity rather than as a time of waiting; sometimes it takes more faith to wait than to walk. And He gave me the grace to wait. As Paul said of his own experience, "Three times I pleaded with the Lord to take [this obstacle] away from me. But he said to me, 'My grace is sufficient for you, for my power is made perfect in weakness' " (2 Corinthians 12:8–9).

Mrs. Charles Cowman, in her beloved book *Streams in the Desert*, said, "Often God delays purposely, and the delay is just as much an answer to your prayer as is the fulfillment when it comes."

As I waited, I found joy in giving—reaching out to my older daughter and sharing in her joy of young marriage and motherhood. God also provided me with other "daughters"; a succession of college-age girls found a home away from home with us.

Though I waited for God to work in areas that were beyond my control, I did not sit and vegetate. As I worked in other portions of God's garden, God was working in my daughter's heart: "He does great things beyond our understanding" (Job 37:5).

I'll never forget that Sunday morning, Mother's Day, when the door between us reopened a crack. In church, she sat on my side of the sanctuary. After the service she came up to me, thrust a card into my hands, quickly hugged me, and swiftly walked away.

In the next few months, if we accidently ran into each other at the shopping center, she spoke rather than turning away from me. Not long after receiving that Mother's Day card, I answered the doorbell and found her waiting at the entrance. Talk about surprise! We had moved that spring and I wasn't even sure she knew where we lived. She needed something that only I could help her with, and she made her request. Though we said little of consequence, I gave her a brief tour of the new house before she left.

Within the next few months she stopped by again, and again, talking a little more each time, sharing her plans for the future. I listened and tried to encourage her. Finally, after two years away, she came to see me at the office where I administrate the work of Overeaters Victorious. In tears she asked if she could come home.

When the question I'd so longed to hear was actually spoken, I had mixed emotions. I'd settled into a peaceful life. Would her presence destroy the calm of our home or of my spirit? Lee and I talked at length. We prayed, asking for guidance. We called a family meeting to discuss potential problems—and solutions. We finally said "yes," we'd give it a try.

All a little older and wiser, it worked this time. For six months we all made adjustments in our living situation, and then we started planning her wedding—a wedding I'd at one time lost hope of attending.

As I look back, I wonder if I would have been prepared to receive my daughter any sooner. I think not, and this only strengthens my trust in the Lord's timing. You see, I needed time to heal from her leaving *and* to prepare my heart for her return. We needed time—for her to become a woman separate from me, her mother. While she did not come home to the same mother; she did not come home the same daughter, either.

How long I had wanted to be a "good mother!" And how little was I prepared to see this dream challenged, or to go through major changes in myself to see God's idea of a good mother fulfilled in our *particular* situation.

This episode with my daughter taught me that God's will can be found in the midst of obstacles and delays. Psalm 37:23 in the King James says, "The steps of a good man are ordered by the Lord." I've read that George Muller wrote, "and the *stops* also," next to this verse in his Bible.

I need that assurance as I face another obstacle.

CHAPTER NINE

The Challenge of Change

A few years ago I experienced terrible physical suffering. My hair was falling out. My skin was like chalk. I had little resistance to disease. I had only enough energy to work until noon. Naps had become a way of life.

I was still teaching seminars throughout the country, but because of my health I could no longer travel alone. After teaching a session I was so exhausted that I could not stay and talk with participants. In addition to being in severe physical crisis, I was on the edge of total emotional collapse.

My weight was slowly creeping up, and finally a doctor gave me an explanation for my condition: The intestinal bypass operation I had had years ago to help me lose weight—it didn't—was causing severe malnourishment. In reality I was dying inch by inch. My weight gain was my body's attempt to fight back against my malnourished condition.

"Lord, My Ministry's at Stake"

Reversing the surgery was recommended as the only possible answer to my severe physical problems. Though the operation would assure my regained health, it would also mean certain weight gain. I, the author of a bestselling book called *Free to Be Thin*, would most certainly not be thin!

I agonized. I prayed. I begged God to spare me what lay ahead. What would happen to my ministry? I had given my life to ministering to overweight people with what I thought was the permanent answer to being fat. Was I wrong? Would God replace me in this ministry?

Before the surgery, I found some comfort in Paul Billheimer's book *Don't Waste Your Sorrows*. I could see that I was not alone in my questions and feeling of loss. He writes:

> Sometimes God permits one of His servants a large measure of spiritual success for many years. He seems to bear a charmed life. Every effort he makes is prospered and blessed. Then God permits him to be overwhelmed with seeming disaster. He is utterly broken. A work of God under his hand perishes with apparent loss to the cause. It is a mystery. But God has a reason.

The days ahead were dark for me. The surgery was painful and the recovery difficult. But eventually my health returned; my hair returned; my energy returned. As anticipated, so did the pounds—though I carefully watched what I ate.

Though I could slow down the weight gain, I couldn't stop it.

At first I continued to fight with God—pleading, crying, praying. "Lord, this is my work for You. My ministry among overweight people is at stake here. God, listen to me." Actually, there were two issues at stake: my ministry and my wish to be at a normal weight for the rest of my life.

Then for a while I gave up. I accepted the fact that I could continue a disciplined and healthy regimen of diet and exercise, but could only ride out the storm as far as the inevitable weight gain went.

William Booth, the founder of the Salvation Army, once said, "The greatness of a man's power is the measure of his surrender." At this point in my life I had to once again learn to surrender, not to the circumstance at hand, but to God. (It's a lesson that one never learns once and for all.)

Within a few months I was fighting back—not fighting the circumstance of gaining weight, but fighting to overcome discouragement, to find new understanding about God's dealings in my life and new understanding about my physical body. My new challenge was not simply to get thin but to live in victory when all the circumstances were defeating.

Though one dream—being thin—was dying, another dream was germinating, getting ready for birth.

God's Gracious Plan

"I cry out to God Most High, to God, who fulfills his purpose for me" (Psalm 57:2).

To see dreams become reality in my life means that I must be ready to *become* rather than achieve. I must be ready to *give* rather than get, to *serve* rather than demand, to *surrender* rather than struggle. To see wishes become reality means that I will change. I will be transformed.

Time and again in my life I've found that through obstacles—problems—God often initiates internal changes in me that bring me closer and closer to the image of His Son. He is fulfilling His purpose for me!

During the most difficult days following my surgery, I realized that I had built an organization that only had a place for the successful—those who fit into the ideal mold of losing two pounds per week, with no regain. In my schema there was no place for the other 95 percent of us to go for encouragement or ministry. What about those of us who'd been faithful to our diets and still were not "successful?"

The question, when brought before the Lord, caught me up short. I gradually realized that a ministry that welcomed only the "successful" was not a ministry at all. Real ministry happens when a person or group consciously creates an atmosphere of *agape* love. It happens when faithfulness is more important than success.

God's Move

Let me tell you, change can be threatening! Since that initial insight, as I have continued to research the topic of overeating and being overweight, I have been shaken to the core; it has reminded me of the word of the Lord in Hebrews 12:26–27: " 'Once more I will shake not only the earth but also the heavens.' " The words "once more" indicate the removing of what can be shaken—that is, created things—so that what cannot be shaken may remain."

God shakes His children again and again, sifting us so that what remains is gold. Though some parts of my teaching have changed, I have been assured that the biblical principles and precepts that have always been the foundation of my ministry have proven to be unshakable.

It is not uncommon for God to work in a person's life by giving direction that he or she should move to a new locale to minister. Record of this is clear in Acts 23:11: "The following night the Lord stood near Paul and said, 'Take courage! As you have testified about me in Jerusalem, so you must also testify in Rome.' "

I've highlighted that verse in my Bible, as it speaks to me personally of God's call to minister to people with a wider range of problems. "You have testified about me in Jerusalem"—in and through *Free to Be Thin*—while you were losing weight, while you were thin, while you were learning to eat in obedience.

"So you must also testify in Rome"—in and through other writings while you are gaining weight; in "fatness"; while eating in obedience with no weight loss; while exercising with no apparent effect.

God has opened my heart to a new sensitivity to the pain of people who struggle to be faithful without visible results of success. Accusers have said that the changes I'm making in the ministry are an attempt to justify my weight gain. But I can say that the opposite is true. Through my own situation, God has pushed me to accept the challenge of growth to a new level of awareness, sensitivity, and compassion.

My friend Pat Prasuhn has encouraged me by quoting back a line she heard me say in a Bible study on diligence: "Change is certain when you give your life to God. Why? Because with God everything *grows*."

Pat adds her own insight, "God desires for us to grow spiritually. But we need to be willing to change! Flexibility involves yielding, adapting, and bending. One man put it this way: 'Blessed are the flexible, for they shall not be broken.' "

There is a good reason why our goals need to be firm but flexible. The Lord has said, "As the heavens are higher than the earth, so are my ways higher than your ways and my thoughts than your thoughts" (Isaiah 55:9).

The Challenge

Whether life-changes come dramatically, in the form of obstacles that seem to be overwhelming, or more gradually, maybe even as a result of reaching your goals and realizing your dreams, they always present challenges. They are big or little transitions that, if faced with faith and courage, are transforming us from what we once were to what we were designed to become. The challenge of change is this: to believe beyond what we did—and who we were—before.

To some people, change—obstacles—brings defeat. But look at the lives of others. I've already mentioned several biblical women who faced obstacles—transitions—and overcame. Joni Eareckson Tada is a real role model of mine. There is someone who faced the reality of a diving accident that left her a quadriplegic. She surrendered her wishes to the Lord, and she took responsibility to use all her resources to make her life have purpose and meaning. To Joni, a wheelchair hasn't been a trap; it has become a ministry. To Joni, change has been a challenge.

People in Process

I do not know all the works that God has designed for the remaining years of my life. I don't know the shape (literally and figuratively) of the person He can most effectively use for His glory. But, like the apostle Paul, I know that I stand "not ashamed, because I know whom I have believed, and am convinced that he is able to guard what I have entrusted to him for that day" (2 Timothy 1:12). The King James Version uses that wonderful word *committed*: "I know whom I have believed, and am persuaded that he is able to keep that which I have committed unto him. . . ." To underscore the point that what was good for him was good for his readers, Paul continues, "What you heard from me, keep as the pattern of sound teaching, with faith and love in Christ Jesus" (v. 13).

The story of my life isn't over. I am a person in process—as are you. As I grow closer to "forever," I and my wishes are becoming. God and I work together—He being committed to me, and I being committed to Him. Based on 2 Corinthians 6:1, I can say that God and I are fellow workers—co-workers on a project that excites me more than I could ever describe.

He's implanted dreams within me; He's guided my steps; He's forgiven my shortcomings. I've submitted to His lordship; I've walked in obedience. When I've failed Him, I've turned back to Him, assured that He and I can continue on from this point, working together on me, becoming more of what I was designed to be—the woman I want to be.

"In all these things we are more than conquerors through him who loved us" (Romans 8:37)!

CHAPTER TEN

Bread for the Journey

In the middle of a spring cleaning or a redecorating project there comes a moment when you survey the room in total chaos and wish you had never begun. You're sure you will never get things in order again. You've already worked so hard, and you've only just begun. You wish you'd never started. In short, you're discouraged.

Discouragement is an age-old reaction to looming obstacles; occasionally discouragement is the obstacle, as our minds turn mole hills into mountains. Before dreams come true, they can look like cardboard boxes stacked in the garage on moving day.

Consider a few Bible stories: The children of Israel became discouraged as they crossed the desert enroute to the Promised Land. Later they became discouraged when they didn't find Canaan all subdivided with houses already built, ready for occupancy.

Joshua prayed one day, "Ah, Sovereign Lord, why did you ever bring this people across the Jordan to deliver us into the hands of the Amorites to destroy us? If only we had been content to stay on the other side of the Jordan!" (Joshua 7:7).

Job became discouraged with his physical torments and loss of family and property; his "comforting" friends didn't bring him much relief. Mary and Martha became discouraged because Jesus did not arrive in time to prevent the death of their brother, and Jesus became discouraged with Mary and Martha because of their lack of faith.

Paul became mightily discouraged: "We were under great pressure . . . so that we despaired even of life. . . . But this happened that we might not rely on ourselves but on God, who raises the dead" (2 Corinthians 1:8–9).

Discouragement, or even the lack of it, is no measure of one's spirituality. Job, Mary and Martha, Jesus, and Paul were people whose lives were founded on faith. As you work toward becoming the person God would have you be, you *will* get discouraged and impatient. You may wish you had a resident encourager beside you to coach and coax you, but more often than not, you will have to encourage yourself.

I shared with you earlier my wish to be more physically fit and my goal to exercise daily. This has been a trouble spot for me all my life. I am not naturally inclined toward being physically active. I enjoy it once I begin, but beginning—that's a real struggle. I often envision one of those fairy-tale wishes: a coach arriving every morning at my house, yanking me out of bed, giving me a positive pep talk, turning on the exercise video, or—

like a drill sergeant—pushing me the two or three miles I need to walk.

But that has not happened. If I get up in the morning and go through an exercise routine or take a walk, it is not because of some other person pushing me to do so; it's because I have learned to get myself going.

Deep within us all is a wish for a lifelong mother—someone whose full-time ministry is to see that we do the things we should and accomplish the things we wish.

Don't get me wrong; I have friends who encourage me, friends who are committed to me and ask, "What are you reading these days? How's your quiet time lately?" These gentle reminders encourage me to continue in those disciplines. But those friends have their own lives to live. They have jobs and responsibilities that have nothing to do with me; they have their own reading to do and their own quiet times to maintain. What's more, they need me to be an encourager for them; I can't expect them to be there every minute for me.

So where do I get the encouragement I need, right when I need it most? From the Spirit who lives within me and from disciplines I place on myself. Encouraging myself is one of the new responsibilities that comes with ratifying my wishes. How do I do it?

From the story of Peter walking on the water, I see that God gives us strength to overcome only as we look for it. If we want an excuse to quit—to drown—we will. Paul said that the Lord's strength was made perfect when he was weak (2

Corinthians 12:9). The Lord's strength—and joy and peace—become mine as I follow these guidelines.

Live in God's Word

Read It Daily

Jesus taught us to pray, "Give us each day our daily bread" (Luke 11:3). He said that He is the Bread of Life; those who come to Him will never hunger or thirst (John 6:35). And when resisting the devil, He said, "Man does not live on bread alone, but on every word that comes from the mouth of God" (Matthew 4:4).

Nutritionists repeatedly point out the physical disadvantages of skipping breakfast. One is that our performance between two and four in the afternoon is directly related to what we ate that morning for breakfast, no matter what we ate for lunch. That is why so many dieters cave in to temptation in the afternoon or while they are preparing dinner.

Those who skip spiritual breakfast—feeding only on what they hear on Christian radio or TV—are like spiritual dieters; they are not ready for the stressful times when they need encouragement.

Speak God's Word to Yourself

"I have hidden your word in my heart that I might not sin against you" (Psalm 119:11). I have learned to paraphrase scripture in the first person *I* and *me*. When I need strength for the journey I read from my journal or cards upon which I have written God's promises to me—as I've inserted my name where appropriate. I put these promises on my car visor, the bathroom mirror, and kitchen cupboards. I love Post-It Notes for attaching verses anywhere, because they don't damage painted surfaces or mark mirrors.

More than once this method of putting God's Word in my heart has saved my life and helped me turn my foot—and my thoughts—from temptation. It has helped me overcome devastating memories and feelings of total failure.

Recently when I was suddenly discouraged about weight gain (the "attack" was triggered by seeing myself in a department-store mirror), I headed for the solitude of my car where I repeated: "Neva, you are God's workmanship. You. Now. Not just when you were thin, but even now, just as you are. I am God's handiwork. I will trust Him. I will obey Him. I will not be ashamed."

I could say this on the basis of Ephesians 2:10: "For we are God's workmanship, created in Christ Jesus to do works which God prepared in advance for us to do." By repeating God's Word, I am able to remind myself of how God sees me (see also Psalm 103).

Another verse that has helped me is Exodus 14:13, Moses' word to the children of Israel: "Do not be afraid. Stand firm and you will see the deliverance the Lord will bring you today. The Egyptians you see today you will never see again."

In the face of my obstacles—like modern-day charging Egyptian chariots—I can repeat Jesus' word to His disciples, "Take courage" (Matthew 14:27).

Meet Frequently with Other Christians

Hebrews 10:24–25 says it all: "Let us consider how we may spur one another on toward love and good deeds. Let us not give up meeting together, as some are in the habit of doing, but let us encourage one another." I couldn't maintain my vital faith if I weren't part of a church, where I can love and be loved; serve and be served; pray and be prayed for.

Nor should you limit yourself—learn to fellowship with others who are not in your church or specific Bible study or prayer group. God has given us a wonderful "body of Christ" that is not limited by the boundaries of denominations or physical walls. I am not encouraging you to be a "church-hopper," just to accept fellowship and encouragement from whomever God chooses to send it.

Give Encouragement

As much as I receive encouragement from others, it's important for me to encourage others. Philippians 2:4 says, "Each of you should look not only to your own interests, but also to the interests of others."

I have discovered that people are often more encouraged by the hope I have in the face of my difficulties, by my determination not to quit, than they are by the victories I have won.

Let others know how God is helping you—and

that He can help them. To be an encouragement to someone else, you don't have to have all the answers or formulas for success. You just need to reach out to them with genuine interest and care. And there's something wonderfully circular about caring for others. As you give encouragement, it comes back around to you.

Pray Consistently

The Scriptures repeat the admonition to draw close to the Lord: "Let everyone who is godly pray to you" (Psalm 32:6); "Pray in the Spirit on all occasions with all kinds of prayers and requests" (Ephesians 6:18); "Pray continually" (1 Thessalonians 5:17).

I don't pray that God will take an obstacle I'm facing away; I pray for strength to be an overcomer. As William Cowper wrote:

> And Satan trembles when he sees,
> the weakest saint upon his knees.

The strength I receive to overcome obstacles and discouragement often comes as I am quiet—restrained in activity and emotionally still—before the Lord:

> This is what the Sovereign Lord, the Holy One of Israel, says:
> "In repentance and rest is your salvation,
> in quietness and trust is your strength."
> —Isaiah 30:15

And Lamentations 3:26 says:

> It is good to wait quietly for the salvation of the Lord.

I know that when I neglect praying, even when I read the Scripture daily, even when I'm around people all day, I get lonely. And to me, loneliness breeds discouragement. I get lonely because I miss talking *and* listening to the Lord.

I need to verbalize my needs and wishes, obstacles and possible solutions, presenting them to the Lord. I need to acknowledge my discouragement and the existence of any obstacles. I know I too often try to deny the first evidence of an upcoming obstacle. Maybe I wish it would go away by itself. Maybe I don't want to expend unnecessary energy. In Mark 6:35 the disciples acknowledged the problem as they saw it: A huge crowd had gathered and they were getting hungry. "This is a remote place, and it's already late in the day," they said. "How are these people going to eat?" They didn't deny the problem at hand; they took it to Jesus before acting on their own solutions.

As much as I need to present my needs to the Lord, I need to listen for the feedback His Holy Spirit speaks to my spirit. My example is Mary, Martha's sister, "who sat at the Lord's feet listening to what he said" (Luke 10:39).

Take Time to Think

As we pray we need to give God time to work in our thoughts. Larry Crabb, in his book *Inside Out*, emphasizes the importance of thinking issues through in the context of a devotional life reverently focused on God's kingly reign over all creation.

In our pressurized society, people who are out of shape mentally usually fall victim to ideas and systems that are destructive to the human spirit and to human relationships. They are victimized because they have not taught themselves how to think; nor have they set themselves to the life-long pursuit of the growth of the mind. Not having the facility of a strong mind, they grow dependent upon the thoughts and opinions of others. Rather than deal with ideas and issues, they reduce themselves to lives full of rules, regulations, and programs.

When we prayerfully deal with open-ended questions and wrestle with ideas that have no easily packaged answers, we begin to pray prayers that go deeper than those in which we try to convince God to see things our way.

Paul shared a wonderful promise for knowing God's will, but it is connected to an exhortation: "Do not conform any longer to the pattern of this world, but be transformed by the renewing of your mind. Then you will be able to test and approve what God's will is—his good, pleasing and perfect will" (Romans 12:2).

Write—and Read—a Journal

As part of my prayer time I write in my journal. I put down my prayer requests, not as a shopping list that God must fill, but as notes of request. I write thank you notes to God for answers to prayer. I write love notes to Him in praise and worship. I write down the ways I've seen Him working in my life.

When I'm particularly discouraged I read portions of my old journals. As the Bible is the account of God's working in the lives of His people, my journals are the account of His working in me.

> I will remember the wonders he has done. (1 Chronicles 16:12)

> I will remember the deeds of the Lord;
> yes, I will remember your miracles of long ago.
> I will meditate on all your works
> and consider all your mighty deeds. (Psalm 77:11–12)

Along a similar line, I hang reminders of wishes that God has helped me turn to reality where I will see them: diplomas, awards, notes from friends, difficult-to-finish craft projects. Many people hang these for others to see; I hang them as a reminder for myself: "We are more than conquerors through him who loved us" (Romans 8:37).

Live in Continual Praise

Many of my friends have taught me the truth of Psalm 35:28: "My tongue will speak of your righteousness and of your praises all day long."

My first lessons in praise came years ago as I was lying in a hospital bed, suffering intensely. An older woman, Bert Peterson, came to visit me, and the sight of her made my eyes fill with tears. She did not react as I expected. She didn't say,

"Oh, Neva dear, I'm so sorry." She said, "Young woman, it is time you learned to live in praise to God." I just looked at her. I was in such terrible pain. "Say it," she said. "Say 'praise God.'"

She repeated the command until I was able to rise above the pain in praise. The pain did not go away, but I became stronger in the midst of it, more able to bear it.

My friend Tom Petherbridge taught me about praising God in conversation. Tom always praises God for the slightest things. I have met others who do the same, but with Tom there is a unique attitude of deep thanksgiving and praise that gives his words credibility.

Dale Tollefson, a manager in a large corporation in the Midwest, taught me about praising God in the work place. He boldly witnesses to others at the office and holds a Bible study for interested co-workers. His example has given me the courage to witness wherever I find the opportunity—and to look for opportunities in ordinary places. And Barb Tollefson, Dale's wife, taught me to praise God in the midst of depression and confusion when she stood with me through some tough days many years ago.

"Through Jesus, let us continually offer to God a sacrifice of praise—the fruit of lips that confess his name" (Hebrews 13:15).

Ephesians 3:20–21 has been a favorite of mine for years:

> Now to him who is able to do immeasurably more than all we ask or imagine, according to his power that is at work within us, to him be glory in the church and in Christ Jesus

throughout all generations, forever and ever!

Yes, His plan for us is a plan that is *more* than we could ask or think. We *can* become more of what we were designed to be as we work together with our Lord, trusting and obeying His direction.

And in the process, let God be glorified, let God be praised. After all, isn't that the deepest wish?

Long-Term Personal Goals Worksheet

"So we make it our goal to please him."
2 CORINTHIANS 5:9

"So we make it our goal to please him."
2 CORINTHIANS 5:9

Family Life
Goal 1: In ____ (number) years I want to _____
_____
_____.

Costs: _____
_____
_____

Possible Solutions: _____
_____
_____

Goal 2: In ____ (number) years I want to _____
_____
_____.

Costs: _____
_____
_____

Spiritual Life
Goal 1: In ____ (number) years I want to _____
_____
_____.

Costs: _____
_____
_____

Possible Solutions: _____
_____
_____

Goal 2: In ____ (number) years I want to _____
_____
_____.

Costs: _____
_____
_____

"So we make it our goal to please him."
2 CORINTHIANS 5:9

Vocation

Goal 1: In ____ (number) years I want to _____
_____
_____ .

Costs: _____
_____
_____

Possible Solutions: _____
_____
_____

Goal 2: In ____ (number) years I want to _____
_____
_____ .

Costs: _____
_____
_____

Christian Ministry

Goal 1: In ____ (number) years I want to _____
_____
_____ .

Costs: _____
_____
_____

Possible Solutions: _____
_____
_____

Goal 2: In ____ (number) years I want to _____
_____
_____ .

Costs: _____
_____
_____

"So we make it our goal to please him."
2 CORINTHIANS 5:9

Hobbies

Goal 1: In _____ (number) years I want to _____
_____
_____ .

Costs: _____
_____
_____

Possible Solutions: _____
_____

Goal 2: In _____ (number) years I want to _____
_____
_____ .

Costs: _____
_____
_____

Physical Health

Goal 1: In _____ (number) years I want to _____
_____
_____ .

Costs: _____
_____
_____

Possible Solutions: _____
_____

Goal 2: In _____ (number) years I want to _____
_____
_____ .

Costs: _____
_____
_____

"So we make it our goal to please him."
2 CORINTHIANS 5:9

Emotional Health

Goal 1: In _____ (number) years I want to _____

_____

_____ .

Costs: _____

_____

_____

Possible Solutions: _____

_____

_____

Goal 2: In _____ (number) years I want to _____

_____

_____ .

Costs: _____

_____

_____

Social Relationships

Goal 1: In _____ (number) years I want to _____

_____

_____ .

Costs: _____

_____

_____

Possible Solutions: _____

_____

_____

Goal 2: In _____ (number) years I want to _____

_____

_____ .

Costs: _____

_____

_____

"So we make it our goal to please him."
2 CORINTHIANS 5:9

Finances

Goal 1: In _____ (number) years I want to _____

_____

_____ .

Costs: _____

_____

Possible Solutions: _____

_____

Goal 2: In _____ (number) years I want to _____

_____

_____ .

Costs: _____

_____

_____

Education

Goal 1: In _____ (number) years I want to _____

_____

_____ .

Costs: _____

_____

Possible Solutions: _____

_____

Goal 2: In _____ (number) years I want to _____

_____

_____ .

Costs: _____

_____

_____

Recommended Reading

Alexander, John W., *Managing Our Work*, InterVarsity Press, Downers Grove, Ill., 1975.

Backus, William, *Finding the Freedom of Self-Control*, Bethany House Publishers, Minneapolis, Minn., 1987.

Barna, George and William Paul McKay, *Vital Signs*, Crossway Books, Westchester, Ill., 1984.

Beattie, Melody, *Codependent No More*, Harper/Hazelden, Center City, Minn., 1987.

Billheimer, Paul E., *Don't Waste Your Sorrows*, Bethany House Publishers, Minneapolis, Minn., 1979.

Blaiklock, E.M., *Today's Handbook of Bible Times and Characters*, Bethany House Publishers, Minneapolis, Minn., 1979.

Bobgan, Martin and Deidra, *Hypnosis and the Christian*, Bethany House Publishers, Minneapolis, Minn., 1984.

Bourke, Dale Hanson, *You Can Make Your Dreams Come True*, Revell, Old Tappan, N.J., 1985.

Bristo, John Temple, *What Paul Really Said About Women*, Harper and Row, New York, 1988.

Coleman, William L., *Today's Handbook of Bible Times and Customs*, Bethany House Publishers, Minneapolis, Minn., 1984.

Conn, Charles Paul, *Making It Happen*, Revell, Old Tappan, N.J., 1981.

Cook, William H., *Success, Motivation and the Scriptures*, Broadman Press, Nashville, Tenn., 1974.

Cowman, Mrs. Charles E., *Streams in the Desert*, Zondervan, Grand Rapids, Mich., 1974.

Crabb, Lawrence J. and Dan B. Allender, *Encouragement: The Key to Caring*, Zondervan, Grand Rapids, Mich., 1984.

Crabb, Larry, *Inside Out*, NavPress, Colorado Springs, Colo., 1988.

Dayton, Edward R. and Ted. W. Engstrom, *Strategy for Living: How to Make the Best Use of Your Time and Abilities*, Regal Books, Ventura, Calif., 1976.

Deen, Edith, *All the Women of the Bible*, Harper and Row, New York, 1955.

Dowling, Colette, *The Cinderella Complex*, Pocket Books, New York, 1981.

Engstrom, Ted and R. Alec MacKenzie, *Managing Your Time*, Zondervan, Grand Rapids, Mich., 1967.

Ezell, Lee, *The Cinderella Syndrome*, Harvest House Publishers, Eugene, Ore., 1985.

Fleming, Jean, *Between Walden and the Whirlwind*, NavPress, Colorado Springs, Colo., 1985.

Foster, Richard, *The Celebration of Discipline*, Harper and Row, New York, 1978.

Gospel Publishing House, *Melodies of Praise*, Gospel Publishing House, Springfield, Mo., 1957.

Gundry, Patricia, *Neither Slave Nor Free*, Harper and Row, New York, 1987.

Haach, Dennis, *The Rest of Success*, InterVarsity Press, Downers Grove, Ill., 1989.

Hills, Dr. Dick, *Not Made for Quitting*, Bethany House Publishers, Minneapolis, Minn., 1973.

Hummel, Charles, *Tyranny of the Urgent*, InterVarsity Press, Downers Grove, Ill., 1967.

Jepsen, Dee, *Women Beyond Equal Rights*, Word Books, Waco, Tex., 1984.

Karssen, Gien, *Her Name Is Woman, Book Two*, NavPress, Colorado Springs, Colo., 1977.

Karssen, Gien, *The Man Who Was Different*, NavPress, Colorado Springs, Colo., 1987.

Kidd, Sue Monk, *God's Joyful Surprise, Finding Yourself Loved*, Harper and Row, New York, 1987.

Lakein, Alan, *How to Get Control of Your Life and Your Time*, Signet, New York, 1973.

LeSourd, Sandra, *The Compulsive Woman*, Chosen Books, Old Tappan, N.J., 1987.

Lindquist, Marie, *Holding Back*, Harper/Hazelden, Center City, Minn., 1987.

Loane, Marcus L., *Godliness and Contentment*, Baker Book House, Grand Rapids, Mich., 1982.

MacDonald, Gordon, *Ordering Your Private World*, Thomas Nelson, Nashville, Tenn., 1985.

MacDonald, Gordon and Gail, *Affirmation and Rebuke*, InterVarsity Press, Downers Grove, Ill., 1986.

Mack, Wayne A., *A Homework Manual for Biblical Counseling*, Presbyterian and Reformed Publishing Company, Phillipsburg, N.J., 1980.

Malcolm, Kari Torjesen, *Women at the Crossroads*, InterVarsity Press, Downers Grove, Ill., 1982.

McConnell, William T., *The Gift of Time: Time in Culture and the Kingdom of God*, InterVarsity Press, Downers Grove, Ill., 1983.

Morgan, G. Campbell, *Handbook for Bible Teachers and Preachers*, Baker Book House, Grand Rapids, Mich., 1982.

Murray, Andrew, *The Believer's Secret of Obedience*, Bethany House Publishers, Minneapolis, Minn., 1982.

Murray, Andrew, *The Master's Indwelling*, Bethany House Publishers, Minneapolis, Minn., 1977.

O'Connor, Elizabeth, *The Eighth Day of Creation*, Word Books, Waco, Tex., 1971.

Ortlund, Anne, *The Disciplines of the Beautiful Woman*, Word Books, Waco, Tex., 1971.

Paul, Jordan, Ph.D. and Margaret Paul, *Do I Have to Give Up Me to Be Loved by You?*, Compcare, Irvine, Calif., 1983.

Penn-Lewis, Jessie, *The Magna Carta of Woman*, Bethany House Publishers, Minneapolis, Minn., 1975.

Porter, Mark, *The Time of Your Life: How to Accomplish All*

That God Wants You to Do, Victor Books, Wheaton, Ill., 1983.

Rinker, Rosalind, *Prayer: Conversing With God*, Zondervan, Grand Rapids, Mich., 1959.

Scanzoni, Letha Dawson and Nancy A. Hardesty, *All We're Meant to Be*, Abingdon Press, Nashville, Tenn., 1986.

Seamands, David A., *Healing of Memories*, Victor Books, Wheaton, Ill., 1985.

Slater, Michael, *Stretcher Bearers*, Regal Books, Ventura, Calif., 1985.

Smedes, Lewis, *Forgive and Forget*, Harper and Row, New York, 1984.

Spencer, Aida Besancon, *Beyond the Curse: Women Called to Ministry*, Thomas Nelson, Nashville, Tenn., 1985.

Steinberger, G., *In the Footprints of the Lamb*, Bethany House Publishers, Minneapolis, Minn., 1986.

Tischler, Nancy M., *A Voice of Her Own*, Zondervan, Grand Rapids, Mich., 1987.

Wright, H. Norman, *Making Peace With Your Past*, Fleming H. Revell, Old Tappan, N.J., 1985